**Custom
Enterprise
.com**

ft.com

Welcome to the next generation of business.

There is a new world which we can look at but we cannot see. Yet within it, the forces of technology and imagination are overturning the way we work and the way we do business.

ft.com is both gateway and guide to this world. We understand it because we are part of it. But we also understand the needs of businesses which are taking their first steps into it, and those still standing hesitantly on the threshold. Above all, we understand that, as with all business challenges, the key to success lies not with the technology itself, but with the people who must use it and manage it. People like you; the future minded.

See a world of business.
Visit us at www.ft.com today.

GABY WIEGRAN • HARDY KOTH

Custom Enterprise .com

Every product

Every price

Every message

ft.com

an imprint of Pearson Education

London • New York • San Francisco • Toronto • Sydney • Tokyo • Singapore • Hong Kong

Cape Town • Madrid • Paris • Milan • Munich • Amsterdam

PEARSON EDUCATION LIMITED

Head Office:
Edinburgh Gate
Harlow CM20 2JE
Tel: +44 (0)1279 623623
Fax: +44 (0)1279 431059

London Office:
128 Long Acre
London WC2E 9AN
Tel: +44 (0)20 7447 2000
Fax: +44 (0)20 7240 5771
Website: www.business-minds.com

First published in Great Britain in 2000

© Pearson Education Limited 2000

The right of Gaby Wiegran and Hardy Koth to be identified as Authors
of this Work has been asserted by them in accordance
with the Copyright, Designs and Patents Act 1988.

ISBN 0 273 64919 1

10 9 8 7 6 5 4 3 2 1

Typeset by Northern Phototypesetting Co. Ltd, Bolton
Printed and bound in Great Britain by Biddles Ltd, Guildford & King's Lynn

The Publishers' policy is to use paper manufactured from sustainable forests.

Contents

Foreword

Survival of the fittest in the digital age

Business evolves much as nature does

Business evolves much as nature does. Charles Darwin's ideas, propounded in 1859, have been compared to any number of social phenomena, but nowhere are they more applicable than in the world of business today. His theory was that species develop variations by chance, but that only some characteristics are well suited to living under continually changing environmental conditions. Only the fittest will survive and be able to reproduce again. This process of variation and selection creates the basis for new species.

Left to nature's timetable, this process usually takes place gradually, too slowly to be observed within a human lifetime. However, man-made environmental changes have provided some vivid examples of how evolution can be accelerated. For thousands of years, white butterflies have been overwhelmingly more common than black ones in England – by a ratio of 1 million to one. Those black butterflies were disadvantaged compared to the white one because, when they rested on the white bark of the trees in middle England, they could be easily spotted by birds, which ate them before they ever had a chance to reproduce.

During the Industrial Revolution, however, conditions changed. By the mid-19th century, the air in parts of Britain was so filled with soot from coal-fired factories that the bark turned black. White butterflies sitting on the black bark were now easy prey while the black butterflies thrived, and within a few years the majority changed from white to black. However, that advantage was temporary – as people became more conscious of their environment and shifted to cleaner energy sources, the majority butterfly population changed once more back to white, through the same evolutionary process. If the species had not had the capability to adapt to these environmental changes quickly it probably would never have survived the Industrial Revolution. The birds, in turn, would have needed to find alternative sources of food or they would not have survived either.

This ecological example shows how a change in the environment can quickly disadvantage some species that have been very successful over a long period of time. Of course, a comparatively small change in the environment, such as polluted air, will lead only to small adaptations, such as a change in colour. However, widespread climatic shifts can have dramatic consequences for all forms of life. An ice age, for example, can fundamentally change the competitive advantages of all species and can even wipe out those that have already been around for millions of years.

These same principles apply to the competitive world of business in a free market economy. Today we are on the threshold of a change that combines the short-term timetable of a man-made environmental change with the permanent and all-pervasive scale of a general climatic shift.

The change is called the World Wide Web and its effects can be thought of in terms of those of a digital ice age. In most quarters, businesses are adapting, as they might in the beginning phases of an ice age, as if coping entailed nothing more than wearing an extra sweater. But it is becoming increasingly clear that more fundamental changes are required.

For those who have looked further ahead, some challenges have presented themselves – in ice age terms, areas that are now deserts may emerge as fertile farmland, while what is now fertile farmland may disappear under glaciers. Forward-looking companies are setting up their business in the desert now but traditional companies are clinging doggedly to their farmland. Those old established businesses must be aware that their current competitive advantage could vanish quickly. Those that sit back and assume that their traditional market strength will go on forever will suffer the fate of the white butterfly. The birds do not care how long they have been around.

Although, admittedly, many successful business models have been developed more or less accidentally, the current climatic changes do not allow us that luxury. Unlike the butterflies, however, we do not have to sit still and wait for our natural predators to pick us off or wait until a new variation or business model emerges by chance. We have the great advantage of being able to develop a strategy deliberately, thus producing a successful new business model. The principle of survival of the fittest remains the same; only in this case, the selection is made primarily not by predators or competitors. Rather, it is made by customers, who, like the birds, are looking for the best deal for themselves.

When there are no major changes in the environment, businesses can usually survive and even thrive by developing innovative products and optimizing processes. The Internet and the World Wide Web, however, constitute such a tremendous change in the environment that new business models have to be developed in order to be successful. Nothing can be left to chance. The danger in the future is not whether a business model will be inefficient but whether it will be irrelevant in the marketplace.

The principle of survival of the fittest remains the same; only in this case, the selection is made primarily not by predators or competitors

In this setting, the art of developing a strategy itself changes fundamentally. Unlike the past, when it was often possible to develop a strategy and then hand it over to information technology people to implement the software component of it, the Internet and the technological possibilities it offers are now at the very heart of every strategy in the web. They have to be integrated into the strategy development from the very beginning if the business is to survive.

January 2000, Dr Rolf W. Habbel
Vice-President, Booz Allen & Hamilton

Acknowledgements

The authors have had the benefit of endless good advice and information in gathering material for this book from many people – they know who they are. Additionally, we want to extend special thanks to a few people who committed their valuable time to make input and comment on the draft or manuscript version of the book:

- Claus Nehmzow for his great ideas in shaping the initial concept of the book

- Jens Niebuhr for his discussions and incisive comments about online auctions and active and passive customization

- Achim Schneider for cross-checking many technical and IT-related details we refer to throughout the book

- Alexander Weigmann for his creative ideas and valuable observations on the book as a whole

- And last, but certainly not least, we would like to thank Gerd Wittkemper, Helmut Meier, Rolf Habbel, Adam Bird and Christiane Döhler for their continuing encouragement, support and striving to attain the highest quality.

Part I

Introduction

Chapter 1

Why customization?

A few hundred years ago every product could be said to have been customized. Mass production had yet to be invented. If you needed a chair, you went to the carpenter and the chair was made according to your specifications. If you needed a pair of shoes, you went to the shoemaker and they were cut to fit your feet. And, if you were willing to pay a higher price to get your shoes sooner, the shoemaker would probably put your neighbours' shoes aside and work on yours first. Even if the product could be

> **A few hundred years ago every product could be said to have been customized. Mass production had yet to be invented**

made in bulk, such as soap, it would still be sold for different prices to different people, on different days and in different villages, with payment often in the form of barter. And the communication with the customer was, of course, very personal, always one to one, and in fact, seller and buyer might know each other very well.

This customized production, pricing and communication changed considerably with the advent of mass production. Products needed to be standardized in order to reap the full benefit of the assembly line. Henry Ford's famous line 'You can have your car in any color as long as it's black' indicates that the preferences of the individual customer were secondary to the need to have standardized features that fitted into the production process. In order to fulfil the needs of most drivers of the day the cars were produced to provide basic transportation, not recreational or luxury travel or to meet individual needs.

Standardization of product features has unquestionably facilitated quantum leaps in the speed and cost of production. Many products that we take for granted today would be expensive and exclusive, would perhaps not exist at any price, were it not for standardization. But standardization has also had other effects that might not be obvious at first sight – effects that have had huge implications for the way in which modern society is organized.

For example, to justify standardized mass production, large production quantities were needed. Once they were produced, those quantities could not be sold only in the vicinity of the factory any more, because there was usually not enough demand. Producers needed to exploit larger markets, first in the county or province, then in the country and, finally, in the whole world. Whole classes of intermediaries sprang up to move the products from factory to customer – traders, merchants, dealers and retailers – and as they did so, the era of direct communication between customer and manufacturer came to an end.

This new system was not without its costs. While production efficiency increased dramatically, and made goods available to vastly larger numbers of people at substantially lower costs, it also had the effect of slowing down the feedback loop between producers and customers. The customer could no longer say to the carpenter that he needed a wider, sturdier chair because he had gained weight, or that one foot was half an inch longer than the other, so could the shoemaker give him a little extra room in that shoe.

The only information that the manufacturer got directly about one particular product was that the volume of his orders was rising or dropping, but he learned nothing about why this was happening. He did not know if orders were falling because the product was too expensive, or if the product features were ill suited to customer needs or tastes. In some cases, the product might be selling but not at levels retailers had hoped, and, as a consequence, retailers stopped ordering to draw down inventory. The reasons are almost infinite. Perhaps the retailer had been forced by a competitor to de-emphasize his products.

In the international marketplace, the problems were compounded. The government of the importing country may have put a tax on his product as part of a policy of import substitution, or any number of other reasons. There were ways to find this out, of course, but it took time and effort, especially in the beginning when communication was still very slow and market research was not yet the fine art it has now become.

Enter the Internet. The Internet offers the opportunity to re-establish the communication loop between manufacturers and customers. It has the potential to put these parties back in the position they were in before the Industrial Revolution, but, in this case, they are not bound by the confines of a village. Their village has literally become the whole world. The manufacturer can now produce for the world market but at the same time communicate with every single one of its end customers through the web.

Enter the Internet

This technology allows the rebirth of customization. The disconnection between manufacturer and customer created by all those layers of intermediation can now be overcome. The manufacturers can use the advantages of a central production line and, at the same time, customize the product and the price for the individual customer.

This is both good and bad news. Those companies that manage to customize their communication, production and pricing to customer needs will be able to reap immense benefits. But it also means that, through the fast feedback cycle and omnipresent communication capabilities, the fight for the survival of the fittest will pick up speed and ferocity.

The current volume is about helping companies to survive in this new environment. It is intended to help companies look beyond the general chill in the air that is accompanying the new 'digital ice age'. This is not a book about dressing more warmly; it is about how to envision a new business model for your company that will help you survive and thrive in the age of eCommerce.

This is not a book about dressing more warmly; it is about how to envision a new business model for your company that will help you survive and thrive in the age of eCommerce

The ultimate objective of any measure described in this book is to create profit through a web site. We will not focus on communities that are run on a non-profit basis or on anything else on the Internet unless it is done with the explicit intention of making money. For any revolutionary infrastructure, there is generally a period in which the profit dynamics of the business proposition may be in doubt, whether that be electrical power, air travel or satellite telephones. The same is true with the

Internet. The road to the ultimate goal of a profitable web site is not necessarily straight. The web site itself does not have to be profitable from Day 1. However, we believe that it is critical to keep the profit goal in mind and not to rely on fate to reveal a profitable solution too far down the road.

We have structured the book to that end.

In Part II, 'Customization as a key success factor', we discuss the potential of the Internet as a new communication and transaction medium for customizing products and services. We also examine the connectivity between different web sites that is one of the key success factors for customization of individual sites.

In Part III we analyze the basic concepts for customization. It is essential to understand your customers' motivations for surfing the web and to use that insight to help identify potential business partners when you want to start a customized business. We also briefly discuss the different options for communicating product or service features via the web, which becomes especially important if you are selling a customized product or service.

The key challenge is to tailor communications to each customer

Parts IV, V and VI go on to discuss options for customizing communication, production and pricing.

Part IV, 'Customized communication': The two-way nature of the web provides companies with a much richer picture of the behaviour of their clients than can be obtained through common offline media. The key challenge is to tailor communications to each customer, concentrating on those pieces of information that are of real value to each relationship. An example of customized communication would be an online supermarket featuring only meatless recipes on its site when a vegetarian signs on.

Part V, 'Customized production': Web interfaces provide customers with an easy-to-use and efficient medium through which to order products tailored to their needs. The key challenge for any player is not simply to offer possibilities for customization in broad strokes, but to offer options that are targeted to specific customers. An example of customized production would be computers that are built according to a customer's individual specifications.

Part VI, 'Customized pricing': Customers have not only different communication and design preferences; they also have significantly different budgets and willingness to pay for the same product. In the Internet age, firms can take advantage of the information-rich interface and try to determine the right price for a specific customer or let the customer choose the price through e-auctions. One of the best publicized examples of customized pricing is online auctions for spare-seat capacity on aeroplanes that allocate these scarce resources to those customers who are willing to pay the most.

Part II

Customization as a key success factor

Chapter 2

Five steps to profitability

Customization has always held potential value for customers. Too often firms have been limited in their ability to customize because their operations were too rigid or because economies of scale precluded variation. High transaction costs limited customizations to large key accounts that could afford greater prices or whose total business was important enough to a firm to justify absorbing additional investment.

The Internet age, however, opens up unparalleled opportunities to customize product design, service design and pricing. Because all information about individual customers is available in a digitized format and communication with the customer is also mostly digitized, the means are available at significantly lower transaction costs. The resulting economies give a firm much greater margin for meeting a larger number of customer preferences and tastes.

Customization is most useful for turning visitors into customers and generating customer loyalty

When you are making preparations for opening a virtual store, you have to think about attracting traffic to your site and converting visitors into paying customers. Then you have to make sure that they come back again, spending more money on your site and buying products that not only generate revenue but also make the web site itself profitable. Customization can be a tool for all five steps, but it is most useful for turning visitors into customers – the so-called conversion rate – and generating customer loyalty.

Traffic

If no one visits when you first open your virtual store, there is no chance that your web presence will ever make money. Therefore, you need a constant stream of new visitors, which means having a sufficient variety of attractive offerings to draw them in. When you are creating traffic you are at the very beginning of the customer relationship. Because you have very little information about the customer, customization for the individual is difficult. However, planning for customization can help you to create traffic because customized web sites generate publicity and lead to a positive word-of-mouth reputation – at least for now, before customization has become the norm.

Conversion

Once you have generated a constant stream of visitors, you have to convert them into paying customers

Once you have generated a constant stream of visitors, you have to convert them into paying customers. Customization can make sure that the exact information of interest for particular customers is displayed on the screen and that these customers will get exactly the products they want. Customization of the communication, the product and the pricing can, therefore, be a great help in increasing the conversion rate.

Loyalty

The next step is to transform the one-purchase-only customer into a loyal customer who keeps coming back to your web site to buy your product or service. Repeat business is as critical on the Internet as it is in any other form of marketing. Loyal customers require no additional marketing or set-up costs, generally provide a higher revenue per purchase, are less sensitive to price and refer your site to their friends. Customer loyalty is especially important in electronic commerce, where the switching costs between different web sites are relatively low. Customizing

> **The next step is to transform the one-purchase-only customer into a loyal customer who keeps coming back to your web site to buy your product or service**

product or service offerings to a customer's individual needs is an effective method for increasing customer loyalty. The more a customer buys from a certain retailer, the more information the retailer has about that customer and the better the retailer can then tailor the product offering to individual needs. The long-heralded 'segment of one', in which product offerings and marketing are adapted to the needs of individual customers, has become a reality. Because alternative different retailers have had no access to the detailed historical information on the customer's preferences and buying behaviour, they will not be able to address their particular needs nearly as well, making it highly likely that the customer will not switch allegiance.

Share of wallet

Once the retailer has convinced the customer to come back and buy again, the next step is to increase the revenue from this customer. Increasing the share of wallet means selling repeatedly to the same customer, and reducing the customer's purchases from competing retailers – online and traditional bricks and mortar – thus increasing revenue without increasing the number of customers. Customization becomes a crucial part of the strategy because the retailer gains the ability to anticipate customer needs and tastes; the retailer is not only ready when the customer is: the retailer can be there *before* the customer is ready. This turns the relationship into something more than a retail relationship. It becomes closer to a partnership, the way an art dealer may be a partner with a collector. Share of customer wallet is not easy to monitor in absolute terms, however, because it is difficult to determine the size of the wallet. Purchases of a single product – say diapers – may tell you very little about the consumer. After all, rich, poor or somewhere in between, anyone with a small child may be buying them. It is only by analyzing diaper purchases in combination with other products that you begin to develop a more complete profile of household spending.

Product margin

Finally, the retailer has to make sure that he sells products or services with high margins. When a retailer offers many different products, some are almost always more profitable than others. To increase profitability, therefore, it is important to monitor the margins of the products a customer is buying and actively to promote the more profitable products; naturally, web site features that point customers to high-margin products are particularly precious. Again, customization can be valuable, because the retailer can focus its cross-selling activities on high-margin products.

When a retailer offers many different products, some are almost always more profitable than others

It is crucial to factor in these five considerations before designing a virtual store; clearly, when a retailer sets out to build a customized web site, specific features must be included. Choices concerning design of the user interface, the underlying database, the content of the web site, the interface with the production facilities and choices of alliances with business partners may be completely different when the retailer is focused on customization from what they would be if the focus of the business were on, say, offering the lowest prices on the web.

Chapter 3

The Internet as a new communication medium

The Internet has attributes that make a difference not merely in degree, but also in kind

Viewed from one perspective, the Internet is merely one more communication and transaction medium like those that have successfully served the same purpose for years, such as letters, telephones and fax machines. It could be argued that it will not have any major impact on the competitive business environment – it's just another tool. However, the Internet has attributes that make a difference not merely in degree, but also in kind. For example, the Internet makes communication and transactions so much faster and cheaper that whole new business models can be built on the basis of that speed.

It could be argued, furthermore, that the time difference in communication between a few seconds on the Internet and a few minutes on the telephone or via fax is not so vitally important. After all, measured by classic accounting means, we usually do not see aggregated transaction costs. They are hidden in the telecommunication bill, employee salaries and the time the customer has to spend to obtain the desired product or service.

To gain a fuller appreciation of the cost advantages of the Internet, we have to look beyond the measures of classic accounting. Transaction costs are basically the cost of information and communication. In order to analyze the effects on customization we will only look at those transaction costs that are most relevant for customization.

Contact costs

These are the costs of finding out where you can get a specific product or service. The Internet significantly reduces contact costs through its worldwide reach and puts an unbelievable amount of information at your fingertips. The desired trading partner, product or service is relatively easy to find through the web compared to searching for it outside the web, especially if the company is in another country.

Contract costs

Because the Internet makes it so much easier for the customer to compare products and prices and to close deals, contract costs are greatly reduced. The implications are most significant for retailers whose greatest competitive strength is their location. If you have been making money by selling certain items more expensively only because there was no one else in a 30-mile radius selling them, the Internet will represent the greatest competitive threat of your life. The same is true for companies that have charged higher prices because customers did not have the time or patience to compare products and prices from manufacturers or retailers. The costs of comparing prices and closing a deal have been reduced through easier access to information and cheap digital communication.

If you have been making money by selling certain items more expensively only because there was no one else in a 30-mile radius selling them, the Internet will represent the greatest competitive threat of your life

The pendulum can swing both ways, of course. Over time, as the number of web sites and choices increases, people will probably grow impatient with comparison shopping on the web as well.

Web-based retailers can build long-term competitive advantage by developing services that increase price transparency, making it easier to compare prices among a variety of sources. In addition, companies with well-established brands should work hard to establish them as strongly on the web as they have in traditional retailing because, as the number of web sites grows and consumers become confused as well as busy, they will gravitate towards names they recognize.

Configuration costs

The information costs of adapting a product to the specific needs of the customer are also significantly reduced for certain products through the capabilities of the Internet. With a digital interface that supports customization and that is directly linked and interconnected within the manufacturer's company, the customer can configure the product to his own needs and tastes. Since all the information is already available in a digital format, it can be directly used in the production process and future customer communications. This is, of course, not possible for all products, but as we will see in a later chapter, the Internet can add significant value to the sales process of quite a number of different industries.

Control costs

The Internet also significantly reduces the costs of verifying that the order has been recorded correctly and where the order stands in the production or delivery process. This is especially important for customized products, because nothing is more annoying than when a product that is ordered especially to satisfy your particular needs arrives at your door and turns out to be wrong. Currently, the customer would have to call a customer service centre to check the status of an order and whether it had been taken down correctly. With the Internet, the customer can log on to check order status and can be routinely updated at very little cost.

The monetary price for the customer is the sum of the cost of manufacture, transaction costs, inventory, shipping and profit. On top of the monetary cost there are also transaction costs on the customer's side. The customer has to invest time in order to obtain information, compare prices, configure the product and wait for delivery. If transaction costs for the customer are lower on the Internet, and there is additional saving through added convenience, the retailer achieves a distinct competitive advantage compared to a retailer who sells the same product for the same price in his bricks and mortar business.

But that is just on the business side. We should also take into account the time and energy saved by the customer through Internet transactions. This additional convenience is part of the customer service equation that can be used to help build customer loyalty; it becomes a positive measure of value in converting visitors into customers and one-time shoppers into regulars.

Book buying via the Internet

Let's us look at how the Internet can reduce transaction costs for buying books, to choose the most prominent and best-developed market. Imagine you have just read a review of a new book in the newspaper and have decided that you want to buy it. In the bricks and mortar world you have to find the nearest bookshop by looking it up in the Yellow Pages or by asking someone where it is. This can be particularly annoying if you happen to read about the book in a Sunday newspaper and there are no stores open nearby. Then, you have to physically go to that bookshop once it is open again, which is the most time-consuming part of the whole buying process.

With Internet shopping, the customer becomes his own customer service representative

In the same time it takes to look up a bookstore in the Yellow Pages, you can log on to Amazon, Barnes & Noble or Borders, to name but three Internet bookstores, order, and pay for your book – although you will have to wait a day or two for delivery. If you are a repeat customer, your vital payment and shipping information are already recorded. The most time-consuming part in this buying process is to boot up the computer and log on to the web, which might take several minutes. Moreover, you can repeat the same transactions from anywhere in the country. No matter where you go, your Internet bookshop is still there, whereas your bricks and mortar store is not.

With Internet shopping, the customer becomes his own customer service representative. He can log on to the web site of the retailer and check if the product has been ordered, if the order has been recorded correctly and if it has been shipped. There is no need for a customer care call centre to answer all these questions. Many customers who would be reluctant to call a call centre to check the status of the order, because of waiting times and because they do not want to bother anyone, will check the web site for reassurance. The retailer can also proactively inform the customer about the different stages by email, thus keeping the customer informed of the whole buying process.

This is not to denigrate the role of the bookstore. The sight of beautifully designed new books arrayed on shelves has charms of its own and is itself a selling tool. You may buy a book in a store that you would never buy online because you can see it, sample it and flip the pages. If you are lucky, there is an informed and well-read sales assistant who can help you when you can only remember that it was a book by that famous author from South America and it had a bright yellow cover. By contrast, Internet technology can direct you to other titles based on your previous choices and the Internet bookshops have other advantages that are hard to duplicate in a traditional store, like reader feedback on books, the capability to search for out-of-print titles, and an incredible number of available titles. And, title for title, if you know what you want, Internet bookstores are pretty hard to beat.

The Internet offers the possibility of communication that is both general and personal

This example shows how the Internet lowers transaction costs with convenience to the customer and it amply illustrates what makes the Internet so special. The other tremendous advantage lies in the fact that all communication and transaction data on the Internet are already available in a digitized format. Imagine customers sending in their capsule book reviews to Amazon by letter instead of email. Someone at the company would have to type them into the computer so everyone else could share them on the web. The costs of digitizing the information would be prohibitive, apart from such costs as postage, paper and envelopes, which would severely limit the number of letters that Amazon would receive in the first place because customers would simply not want to go through the whole procedure.

The Internet also offers new opportunities for retailers to communicate with customers. While communication through letters, faxes or the telephone can be either very general or very personal, they have both costs and limitations. Direct mail, for example, is based on the broadest categories of affinity – the purchase of mailing lists. Telephone calls – done one at a time – are very time consuming for the company and usually not very focused either, because there is little digitized customer information to personalize the calls. Direct mail usually ends up in the garbage bin. And phone calls from companies you already do business with, let alone 'cold' calls from telemarketers, are generally regarded as a nuisance.

The Internet offers the possibility of communication that is both general and personal. Email is a broad and inexpensive communication medium that can be personalized, based on the digitized information that the retailer has about the customer. The messages conveyed are based primarily on information that the consumer has already volunteered and that is already digitized, which becomes especially important when developing customization concepts.

The unique features of the Internet make it a fast, inexpensive, clean communication and transaction medium for digitized and customized information, in addition to the fact that it can also convey certain digitized goods such as music, newspapers, software or videos directly. The new communication and transaction opportunities do not by themselves constitute a new business model. But the fact that this communication medium exists opens a wealth of opportunities to create new business models based on fast, cheap, digitized and customized communication.

Email is a broad and inexpensive communication medium that can be personalized, based on the digitized information that the retailer has about the customer

So far, most of the successful companies on the web are those whose business model has been easy to adapt to the Internet. For example, when the Internet started to become known to the general public, Dell Computers (***www.dell.com***) was already successfully selling custom-made computers without the Internet all over the world. Dell's existing business model was very easy to adapt to the Internet since the whole customized production and delivery process was already in place. It only had to design a customer interface to bring its business on to the web. As yet, however, the actual potential of new business models on the web has not been fully realized because many web capabilities bear little relation to existing business models and are thus more difficult to recognize and, therefore, to utilize.

virtual visit

Chapter 4

Connections within the web as a success factor

What is the World Wide Web?

So far we have seen how the Internet facilitates communication and transactions between customers and companies because the flow of information is faster, cheaper and digitized. But why is the whole thing called the World Wide Web? The name not only describes the physical structure of a web, but is also a metaphor for the linkages between web sites, companies and customers.

Many web sites in existence today are very similar to companies in the bricks and mortar world. There are Internet bookshops, Internet travel agents and Internet grocery stores, each representing one part of a larger value chain that extends from supplier to manufacturer to wholesaler to retailer to consumer. The way the value chain is segmented from one link to another has remained largely the same, except that some of the retailing has now been shifted to the web. This is natural during the first stage of a developing medium, but it does not have to remain that way and is not likely to.

We can see that the way work is divided between different companies today is not necessarily the optimum in the light of the new communication media

We can see that the way work is divided between different companies today is not necessarily the optimum in the light of the new communication media. Since the Internet significantly changes transaction costs we can expect to see considerable changes in the size of companies and in the tasks that are performed within one company.

As the web develops, the essential structure of companies, their size, functions, average lifetime, pricing and financing, will be challenged. All these things have developed at least partly to overcome the physical limitations of geographical distance and transaction costs. As those limitations are eliminated by the Internet, the structures we thought were fundamental are being shown to be less necessary.

On the web, the lines between one company and another are becoming less important. The physical acts that lie behind a sale to a customer – design, building, shipping and so on – may become less important than managing the flow of information essential to the process. One company in the value chain that performs this function particularly well may take that function over from others. Or it may be some completely external entity. In the future it might no longer be companies as legal entities that succeed but those that integrate the flow of information in the value chains within and between companies. And yet, the customer will see none of it. A customer does not care where one company ends and another starts – he has got a need that he wants met.

A customer does not care where one company ends and another starts – he has got a need that he wants met

Say you want to go on vacation. There are many things you would have to consider before you can actually make a reservation for a flight or hotel. Which country do you want to visit? Is April a good time to go diving in Thailand? What effect did El Niño have on the coral reefs? What is the current political situation? Do you have to take malaria prophylaxis six weeks in advance? Is it a good country for travel with small children? Which airline offers seats where you can lie down and have a good night's rest?

You can obtain that information from different sources – TV, travel guides, travel agents, the tourism office, or friends who have already been there. If you are really lucky the travel agent you select has already been to that country and might be able to answer your questions. But you are taking chances, even if you get lucky once or twice. Basically, you have to do the hard part yourself – obtain all that information before you go to a travel agent. Currently, the value added by the travel agent is not to help you plan but to select the least expensive package for you out of a maze of different pricing models of airlines and hotels.

Part of a successful Internet strategy is the integration of whole value chains within and between companies into one communication flow. The result is an eCommerce service that focuses on customer desires, needs and problems. For our example of travel to Thailand, this would mean that the new Internet travel agent would provide all the information necessary to decide upon a holiday destination by the linkage of critical web sites.

To provide detailed information about the country, political situation, sports facilities, hotel and flight availability, medical advice and more for all holiday destinations in all the countries of the world seems like an impossible task. But it is not. The travel agent does not have to provide all the information himself. Even in the early stages of the Internet most of the information required is already available somewhere. But it is spread throughout the whole web and not everyone has the time and tenacity to search for it. So the next development stage of the web will be not only to provide theoretical access to information through a physical web but also to interconnect the different parts in a meaningful way. There are three stages of information integration.

> **Part of a successful Internet strategy is the integration of whole value chains within and between companies into one communication flow**

Physical connection

The first stage is to establish a physical connection between different pieces of information to make them accessible through a unified platform. The Internet has already reached this standard through the creation of the World Wide Web and the Internet protocol. Protocols and

Even in the early stages of the Internet most of the information required is already available somewhere

formats such as TCP/IP, HTTP and HTML allow various networks to interconnect and various information repositories to be interlinked. Java is another example of an open programming language that runs on various platforms and operating systems.

Logical connection

The second stage is to create logical connections within the web between pieces of information that are related to each other. The first efforts in this direction are hyperlinks between different web sites. An example would be the web site of a travel agent that includes books on travel destinations with a hyperlink to online booksellers. Another hyperlink would be to travel medical sites where vaccination requirements for various destinations are listed. Some businesses have been quick to embrace the logic of these linkages. For example, Amazon supports the creation of hyperlinks through its affiliate programme, where the web site that transfers the customer gets a share of the revenue received at Amazon. Others have so far been slow to integrate their services seamlessly into such customer-centric service offerings. However, once the connections are made and the customer has arrived at the desired web site he will have to fill out yet another questionnaire with all the same information already entered elsewhere. For example, when you perform a search in the search engine AltaVista (**www.altavista.com**) about Arabian horses there is a banner informing you that Amazon sells books about Arabian horses. When you click through to Amazon, however, you do not go directly to books about Arabian horses, as you might expect, but find yourself on the Amazon homepage and must once more key in what you want. A step is missing.

Amazon supports the creation of hyperlinks through its affiliate programme, where the web site that transfers the customer gets a share of the revenue received at Amazon

virtual visit

Seamless integration

The third stage is the seamless integration of information across several web sites. Instead of just linking different sites the information is actually formatted in such a way that it can be transferred between different web sites. For the user it becomes largely indistinguishable where one web site ends and another one starts. The seamless integration can be compared to the software integration between programs such as Microsoft Excel and Microsoft Windows. When you are working in Excel you do not have to know, and probably do not care, whether a certain function, say file saving, is run by Excel or Windows – as long as it saves your file. Extended Markup Language (XML) is an example of technology that will allow you to standardize information so that it will be easier to convey from one web site to another, with a minimum of rekeying.

> **Information is actually formatted in such a way that it can be transferred between different web sites**

Continuing with our example of the intrepid traveller, this would mean that the user can obtain airline information, vaccination information and political information through a series of interconnected web sites without necessarily knowing that he has left the travel agent's site at all. Seamless integration means that all relevant information that the user has already entered will automatically be transferred to the next web site. So when the user is transferred from the travel agent's site to the site of a medical association, the new web site already knows that the user wants to fly to Thailand for 11 days in September and go diving in Phuket. It can thus immediately prompt whether malaria prophylaxis is advisable or not.

Not only can information about the desires of the customer be integrated between web sites but so, too, can the capability to execute various transactions without entering all the personal and payment information again for each new partner. American Express (Amex), for example, will register a credit card customer participating in the Amex loyalty programme with the frequent flier programmes of all participating airlines. This saves the customer the hassle of having to go through the process of applying to all those programmes separately and entering the same information several times, although, obviously, any personal

> **Seamless integration means that all relevant information that the user has already entered will automatically be transferred to the next web site ... [This] requires more initial effort than merely creating hyperlinks**

or transactional information should only be given to third parties with the customer's explicit consent.

The seamless integration of information requires much more initial effort than merely creating hyperlinks. The interface between the two web sites and the transferred data has to be clearly defined. Once these initial requirements are fulfilled, however, every party only has to maintain its own web site and ensure at the same time that the whole integrated network is also up to date.

There are definite advantages to acting quickly to secure the best partners for cooperation. For example, if a travel agent starts an exclusive arrangement with 'Lonely Planet', the world's leading publisher of independent travel guides, competing travel agents will no longer have that option. Even with non-exclusive relationships, it is unlikely that a company will be inclined to enter into strategic relationships with many different partners. A thoughtful and ambitious travel agent could define the standards that a potential partner needs to fulfil to become part of the integrated web. Over time, more and more partners might join, but they would have to meet the high standards laid down at the beginning, providing a degree of quality control that might become part of a brand identity. Hotels could add video clippings of their premises and availability information for bookings, motor home rental companies could add inside views of their campers and national tourist associations could add information about special festivals in their countries.

Through the seamless integration of information, virtual companies can evolve that might look to the customer like one company, but are actually independents, operating behind a unified facade. The key success factor is to create a network of web sites that, in combination, will satisfy customers' needs, regardless of who creates and maintains the different parts of the site. Models and techniques for customization are described in a later chapter and the proposed tasks may seem insurmountable for your own company; but do remember, there is always the possibility of joining forces with others through a virtual company.

The key success factor is to create a network of web sites that, in combination, will satisfy customers' needs, regardless of who creates and maintains the different parts of the site

The more web sites that are connected through seamless information interchange, the more valuable it becomes for others to join. This is known as the 'law of increasing returns', which means that the value of each web site increases exponentially when it is connected with other sites with integrated information and transaction flow.

A simple example shows how the law of increasing returns works. When the first telephone was produced it had little value because there was no one to call. Therefore, there was no incentive for others to buy phone service. As time went on, however, the value of the individual telephone increased because there were more people to call. At the same time prices for manufacturing the device itself and the price for using the lines dropped, because more people were using them. So the costs of phone service were lower, and, at the same time, its usefulness had increased. This beneficial circle continued inexorably and picked up speed until essentially everyone in the industrialized world had a telephone. This same process has held true for every network device, where the usefulness of the individual device is based on communication with others – fax, telex, mail and email.

The law of increasing returns will make sure that more and more people and companies join the web, which will, in turn, support further increases in the number of web sites that are connected through seamless information flow. Of course, the interconnection of web sites with integrated information flow would be a lot easier if there were a common standard for information interchange. Currently, a hotel that wants to be part of several travel agents' web sites might have to program several different interfaces, which certainly does not make the management and maintenance of a web site easier. Those who start to define their web site-specific standards now, however, have the chance to lay the foundation for a de facto standard that could quickly become the basis for information interchange.

> **The law of increasing returns will make sure that more and more people and companies join the web, which will, in turn, support further increases in the number of web sites that are connected through seamless information flow**

So far we have only looked at seamless flow of information between companies. However, to reap the full potential of the Internet, integration of the information generated in the web *within* companies is just as important. Seamless integration of information in the Internet increases revenue through higher customer convenience and helps to reduce costs because part of the work is outsourced to the customer. When this information is integrated with the company's own Intranet, the seamless flow reduces the costs to serve the customer. This efficiency makes the customization of communication, product and price economically feasible.

> **Every business should recognize that the Internet is not just another sales channel that can be added to the existing organization without regard for the implications for the entire organization**

Every business should recognize that the Internet is not just another sales channel that can be added to the existing organization without regard for the implications for the entire organization. Those that do will be under severe pressures from competitors that do recognize this factor, or new companies that are conceived exclusively for the Internet. A surprisingly high number of companies have created web sites that allow online ordering, but have not integrated the system with their internal IT systems, so when a customer orders via the web, the order is printed out in the order entry department and manually entered into the internal order entry systems. This approach might work when a web site is new, but, in the long run, is not sustainable for higher volumes.

The company that has not redesigned its internal processes and IT structure to the demands of the new medium will suffer. The expense of maintaining these multiple internal processes by itself will be a handicap because the higher overhead will preclude the ability to lower prices. But the real long-term handicap will be the company's inability to achieve additional functionality, such as online stock inspection, exact delivery timing and customized communication. As we will see later in this book, integrated internal processes are indispensable to offering customized products and services.

Part III

Basic concepts for customization

Chapter 5

Options for initial consideration

Before you can start to develop a web business based on customization you must consider several things. First, you need a business model that determines what you are trying to sell or how you are trying to make money. There are various options available.

Product

You can sell either a product or a service through the web. Examples are Amazon for selling books or The Wall Street Journal (***www.wsj.com***) for selling information.

virtual visit

Commission

You can make money by serving as a marketplace and live on the commissions from the sales of others. An example would be eBay, which provides a platform for online consumer auctions. eBay receives a small fee for hosting the auction and a percentage of the highest bids.

Advertisements

You can also profit from the high volume of traffic at your site by selling advertisements that are viewed by everyone who visits. Once you have secured high traffic by providing highly desirable information at no cost, or by providing forums for exchanging ideas or for playing games, you can start to market the traffic. An example is Gamesville (***www.gamesville.com***), a purely advertiser-supported web site where people can play games against each other free of charge and win cash prizes, paid for by the revenue generated by the advertisements. The more you know about the people on your web site, the more focused and customized the advertising can become. Customized links are less annoying for the potential customer, because they address his needs. They also generate higher revenues because the advertising commands a higher price.

> **Customized links are less annoying for the potential customer, because they address his needs**

Of course, combinations of product, commission and advertising models are possible, and in practice it is not always easy or necessary to distinguish clearly between them. Many web sites that started out by offering a product or service have now generated so much traffic and collected so much information about their customers that they have begun to sell advertisements or customized links without alienating their original customer base. There are several concepts that need to be considered, which are dealt with in the remainder of Part III.

> **The more you know about the people on your web site, the more focused and customized the advertising can become**

First of all, to be able to design a business model that will continually attract a large number of visitors, and eventually convert them to customers, the company has to learn why people frequent its web site in the first place.

Second, the company has to be able to identify the people it is dealing with because otherwise there is no basis for customization. Only when the company knows who a visitor or customer is, what his preferences are, and what he has previously bought can communication, product features and pricing be adapted to his needs.

And finally, if the business model is built on selling a product or service, the company has to be able to communicate effectively the features of its customized products or services via the web, because otherwise the customer will not buy.

Chapter 6

Motivations for surfing the web

Why surf?

Why do people spend time surfing the Internet? The reasons are probably infinite, but we find that they generally fall under a number of headings that are relevant for designing the customer interface and the whole value proposition for the digital business model. If you have no idea what people are looking for on your web site, how can you choose which options and features you want to include?

If you have no idea what people are looking for on your web site, how can you choose which options and features you want to include?

Every consumer choice is motivated by one of two basic factors: either because a person wants to achieve a certain result or because the activity itself is enjoyable. Depending on the preferences of the individual person, almost any human activity can serve one purpose or the other.

Some people enjoy shopping whether they buy something or not. Whether they go home without buying anything or end up carting home something they had not planned to purchase, the result is secondary to the good time they had wandering around the stores. Others hate shopping and only go to the store to grab something they need quickly. If they come back empty-handed, they have, by their standards, wasted their time.

Some people enjoy shopping whether they buy something or not

The same considerations are also true for Internet shopping. Some enjoy surfing the web itself, whereas others only log on for long enough to be able to do their business. These types can be called, respectively, the 'fun surfer' and the 'convenience surfer'. And there is rarely a pure version of either; someone who buys a new tie after endless harassment from friends and colleagues may blissfully spend the whole afternoon looking for books.

The fun surfer

For the fun surfer, the Internet opens up new opportunities, possibilities and joys. The word 'surfing' itself already suggests that the activity is enjoyable in itself. Give them hours in front of their computer screens every night to surf the web after the stores close and the possibilities are endless. Fun surfers are fascinated by new features, new pieces of information and the new communication possibilities presented by the Internet. Most of this fascination is probably because the medium is new and there is a constant profusion of new web sites to explore. There is also a certain thrill from interacting with strangers, such as playing a game in Gamesville against other players from, say, Moscow or Tokyo.

Fun surfers are a risky bunch to build your business on

Nowadays, most Internet habitués are probably fun surfers. This would also explain why a lot of traffic on a particular site does not necessarily translate into a high number of purchases. Because they find the activity itself enjoyable, they are not the user group that simply must buy something to make the surfing worthwhile. So, if your business model focuses on attracting fun surfers and has a lot of fancy features that do not relate to the buying or decision-making process, you will need a concept of how to make money from the fun surfers.

Obviously, if your web business is built on selling products or services, or on providing a marketplace and living on commissions, you are not going to make any money unless someone eventually buys something. Even if your business model is built on selling the traffic by integrating banner ads into the site, if your visitors do not buy the advertised products, companies will stop buying ads. In short, fun surfers are a risky bunch to build your business on.

'Community surfers'

A subset of fun surfers are the 'community surfers'. They especially enjoy communicating with others. They enjoy being part of a community, helping others, exchanging ideas with experts, or otherwise communing with people who share special interests that may be scarce in their own social milieu. Some also like to show off their own know-how and capabilities within the community – instant intellectual gratification. Although community surfers may not necessarily buy anything on a web site, they can still be very valuable to the site because their feedback and input can be used to enhance the content, making the site more attractive to other visitors who are more inclined to buy.

The convenience surfer

This is the person who surfs the web to obtain information or buy a product quickly. He does not find the experience of surfing the web particularly enjoyable in itself and is driven by achieving results. He is mainly motivated by lower transaction costs in the Internet and wants to avoid unfriendly sales people, traffic jams and cash register queues, endless telephone calls and restricted hours of business.

In fact, convenience surfers should probably not even be called surfers at all because the word 'surfing' sounds like too much fun, but we use the word for everyone online, jolly or not.

Customer time has to be factored into Internet pricing

As we outlined early on in this book, customer time has to be factored into Internet pricing. Saving time is equal to saving money when you consider a customer's total efforts to obtain information and compare prices, and the physical act of shopping. The value is different for every individual. The person

For some, low prices will be everything, no matter how much time they spend trying to find them

who implicitly sets a high hourly rate to his own time is probably very busy with a high income and little free time (or someone who thinks he is really important).

At one extreme, in the case of, say, an investment banker, it might actually be cheaper to employ a personal shopper, who makes all the decisions about what to buy, than to sign on to the Internet. At the other extreme, a person who is unemployed and has lots of time but little money would set a lower hourly rate to his own time. He might spend hours on public transportation to go all over town looking for bargains. And he probably has no Internet access, either.

Obviously, the average Internet surfer does not occupy either of these extremes. The biggest time saving, at whatever rate, probably involves not leaving the house to go to a store. So when you are catering to the convenience surfer you are automatically selecting a certain target group with specific traits that can be weighed in evaluating pricing characteristics. For some, low prices will be everything, no matter how much time they spend trying to find them. For others,

Convenience is a rare commodity on the web

higher prices will not be as costly as the time they have to spend shopping – for these people, convenience is worth higher prices.

At the time of writing, convenience is a rare commodity on the web. This is not a problem for the fun surfer, who may also have a high income and little free time, but because he finds surfing enjoyable in itself, the time he spends on the web would not be considered part of his transaction costs. Therefore, lower transaction costs would not be an incentive.

There are many reasons why convenience is scarce. The Internet is still in its infancy and even arriving at the right web site can be problematical. Convenience surfers have little patience with software problems, long download times and confusing search engines. Those who survive this labyrinth and arrive at the right web sites may find them so complicated and slow and the directions so hard to understand that novices may easily be put off.

Let us return to our travel agent. Imagine that you want to book a flight from London to Bangkok. An integrated travel web site that will allow you to select your flight from different airlines, then automatically use your data to apply for a visa and give you medical information about vaccination requirements does not yet exist. The standard travel web site will allow you to book your flight, but there is little additional convenience beyond what can probably be provided by any bricks and mortar travel agent over the phone.

The second reason for the shortage of convenience surfers on the web is that many possible future convenience surfers like our investment banker have probably not even been on to the web or found the sites that would actually save them time. But their numbers are increasing as some have begun convenience surfing as part of their job; eventually, the critical mass will lead to a point of increasing returns.

> **The Internet is still in its infancy and even arriving at the right web site can be problematical**

An extreme example of a business-to-business web site that ruthlessly focuses on convenience without frills is National Semiconductor, which builds chips that are used in a variety of devices from cellular phones to dishwashers (***www.national.com***). This site is built especially to increase the convenience of a particular customer group, the design engineers for the companies that build the appliances. National Semiconductor conducted several surveys and found out that design engineers were pure convenience surfers. They had a job to do and wanted to get the information quickly and without frills. So the National Semiconductor site has no fancy graphics and colourful pages. Instead it allows the user to search a database of over 20,000 different devices to find the desired chip quickly. The engineer can then order a sample or download a datasheet.

> **Eventually, the critical mass will lead to a point of increasing returns**

Two years after the site went online over half a million engineers worldwide were using it every month. They spend very little time on the site, viewing an average of only two to three pages. Additional graphics would actually decrease the value of the site for the engineers because they offer little additional value, but would considerably increase download times. They would undoubtedly make the site more interesting for the occasional fun surfer, but they are not National Semiconductor customers. Some people would even argue that this is not a web site at all but a database that is made available through the web. But it proves that a successful web site does not have to look like entertainment. It all depends on who your focus customers are.

An example of how convenience does play on the consumer side is in the competition between music retailers Music Boulevard and CD Now. Music Boulevard had so many features

virtual visit

– CD cover art, recommendations, cross references, music trivia, and audio sampling – that consumers trying desperately to catch up on last-minute holiday shopping lost patience with it. For them, the art-light, type-heavy, straightforward CD Now made much more sense.

A successful web site does not have to look like entertainment

The differentiation between fun surfers and convenience surfers does not mean that the fun group are all hippies and the convenience group all Scrooges. But the focus of the web sites is different. Web sites can be optimally designed to cater to both fun and convenience surfer simultaneously. Features can be combined where it is economically and technically possible; sometime, however, choices must be made.

Web site design

Web site design is very similar to product design. Without a clear target group in mind it is difficult to make the right choices. A fun car for single people, for example, will entail a trendier, sportier design than one for a family of five. It is difficult to design a trendy convertible that will accommodate both a pram and 12 bags of groceries in the boot. You have to make a choice between design and practicality. The sports car buyer will probably not see the small boot as an exceptionally positive feature of his car but as long as he can get two suitcases into it for a country weekend with a friend, lack of space is less important than other features. The same type of thinking must go into planning a web site.

You have to make a choice between design and practicality

It is, of course, possible to design a successful web site without a specific target group in mind, but it means taking chances instead of developing a strategy. Some people have a very clear target audience in mind when designing their web site even if they have no elaborate documentation. These are usually the one-man startup companies where the owner has a special interest and designs the web site according to his personal knowledge and enthusiasm. If someone transfers a bricks and mortar business to the Internet he also usually has a pretty clear idea who his target audience is – basically, the same people as in the established business.

However, if someone is designing a new business model for the Internet that does not exist already in the bricks and mortar world, analysis of the target audience is crucial to determine the right mix of convenience and fun. The tendency is, of course, that in the business-to-business market, the main user group will be convenience surfers, whereas in the business-to-consumer and consumer-to-consumer markets both motivations can be relevant.

You have to find out as much as possible about your customer if you want to customize your communication, product, service or pricing. If you do not know who you are dealing with, you cannot individualize your service.

Chapter 7

Identification of business partners

If you want to do customized business on the web, you have to figure out a way to identify your business partners when they log on to your site. Uncertainty poses two problems. Any exchange of information, goods or money becomes difficult if you do not know whether you can work with or trust the other party. This is the foundation of any transaction. And customization becomes very difficult if you have no way of identifying the customer you are dealing with. In this chapter we analyze various tools that can be used to identify your business partner as a basis for transactions and as a basis for customization.

Identification as a basis for transactions

In order to identify your partner as a basis for doing business, you need to know if the other person or company will deliver the product or pay the bill, as you would in any other model of business. Do not cut corners when you are trying to verify whether your partners are trustworthy just because you can make a quick deal on the Internet. The Internet market moves quickly, but

The Internet market moves quickly, but speed does not justify suspension of sound business judgment

speed does not justify suspension of sound business judgment. If they do not deliver the product or pay the bill as promised, you have to know exactly who you are dealing with to have any recourse in law. There are different types of identification that serve this purpose: the concepts of absolute certification, relative certification, reputation and the use of trusted third parties.

Absolute certification

In the bricks and mortar world people usually rely on passports, driver's licences or identity cards that are issued by governments. There are official bodies that issue certificates that will unambiguously identify a person and the pieces of paper are a tremendous advantage.

Unfortunately, such documents are not well suited for use on the Internet. They cannot usually be communicated very well in a digital format. In addition, they are different in every country, which makes identification of customers or companies from countries other than your

Taking legal action against a person in another country is usually very complicated, tedious and costly

own even more difficult. Also, they tell you only who the other person is, giving no indication of reliability or credit-worthiness. If you have a legal contract with your business partner and have identified that business partner as such through a government certificate, but he does not fulfil the contract, you can take legal action against him. It is critical that the contract be written and duly executed – orders received via the Internet might not be considered legal contracts in all countries of the world.

That is the theory, of course. There exists, however, an enormous gulf between the letter of a contract and its enforcement. Taking legal action against a person in another country is usually very complicated, tedious and costly. Most companies do not want to waste their resources fighting legal battles around the globe. Even within your own country the legal contract can be practically unenforceable if the value in dispute is small. Since the greatest number of Internet transactions involve relatively small amounts, lawsuits will, in most cases, cost you much more than you would possibly gain.

In the bricks and mortar world smaller transactions are usually executed 'cash over the counter'. If you want to buy a pair of shoes, the shoe retailer does not have to trust you because, unless you pay, he is not going to let you walk away with the shoes. By the same token, you do not have to trust the shoe retailer either, because if he does not hand over the shoes you are obviously not going to pay. Trust is not necessary to execute the sale successfully. These smaller transactions are normally executed simultaneously, with the buyer, the seller, the cash and the goods in the same place at the same time. On the Internet, however, buyer and seller are usually not in the same place and cannot exchange product and payment at the same time. Therefore, there is a need not only to identify the business partner, but to make sure that he will adhere to the contract.

The risk of the transaction is transferred from the retailer to the credit card issuer, which usually absorbs all but a small fraction of fraud loss

If it is not possible to get the product and the money to the right place at the right time, other solutions to problems of security and trust are necessary. Credit card purchases are widely used on the Internet and give sellers assurance of payment. Credit cards imply a link to the kind of official verification carried by a passport or identity card because you can only get a credit card if you can identify yourself to the issuing bank or other financial institution. At the same time credit cards are widely used in almost every country and therefore already have a big advantage compared to individual countries' passports. Most important, of course, credit cards also assure that the other party will actually pay, and can therefore also be used for smaller transactions, where legal enforcement is practically impossible.

Although credit cards are already widely used on the Internet, they are not particularly well suited for digital payment because of their fundamental lack of security. Today you can buy almost anything on the Internet by giving your credit card number to the seller via the web. The seller will charge the amount to your card and send you the purchased goods. Your card number is no secret, however. Any retailer where you have ever used your card has your number.

In one sense, your credit card is less secure on the Internet than in face-to-face transactions, since the security mechanism of credit cards has always relied on your signature on the slip matching the one on the card. In order to do that, you, your credit card and the retailer have to be at the same place at the same time, which is not possible on the Internet. Even if you sign a credit card authorization and send it to the retailer by mail, this does not help. The retailer now has the signature and the credit card number, but since he still does not have the card itself, he has nothing to compare the signature with. The system seems to work quite well, however, because the risk of the transaction is transferred from the retailer to the credit card issuer, which usually absorbs all but a small fraction of fraud loss.

Private entities now take over functions that have previously been performed exclusively by governments

A real solution to the problem of payment on the Internet can only be offered by digital certificates – digital equivalents of passports or identity cards that could be issued either by governments or by internationally recognized companies. One example is an initiative by Chase Bankers Trust and Deutsche Bank. They have created Identrus to identify people across all web sites and provide information about creditworthiness. This is an example of a tendency we can find all over the web: private entities now take over functions that have previously been performed exclusively by governments, such as identification and supplying means of payment.

Relative certification

Although an absolute certification of Internet users would be reassuring, none is currently available on a broad scale. Therefore, many web sites and business partners have to rely on their own means of certification, or 'relative certification', that are only valid on the individual web site.

Since eBay is only an intermediary, the actual selling and buying is done directly, consumer to consumer

eBay, the auction company we described earlier (*www.ebay.com*), has developed an interesting way of certifying people trading on its site. Since eBay is only an intermediary, the actual selling and buying is done directly, consumer to consumer. This obviously poses some security risks. Suppose a customer in Florida has auctioned a used laptop computer for $800 and the highest bidder lives in San Francisco. The computer has somehow to get to San Francisco and the money to Florida. eBay is no longer involved in the transaction and therefore will make no guarantee that both of the trading parties will actually fulfil the contract. Contrariwise, it would obviously have a negative effect on eBay's business if fraud were common.

In order to secure the basis of its business, eBay has developed a local certification mechanism on its web site that allows users to see the track record of other users. When an item is auctioned, the buyer and the seller can give feedback about the way the transaction was executed. Those comments are made available to all users and are the basis for the eBay rating.

virtual visit

For each transaction, the buyer and the seller get one point each. If they get a good feedback comment by the buyer for instance 'product arrived within three days and was exactly as described', the seller would get one positive point. If the seller's feedback is bad, for example 'cheque did not clear', the buyer would get one negative point. The sum of all positive and negative points is the rating of a particular person. Scores of 30 or 40 positive points are common, although some participants, who are probably selling their goods commercially, have reached ratings of over 5,000.

Normally, the buyer has to send the money first and as soon as the cheque has cleared, the seller sends the item. Thus, the buyer bears the risk. If the item never arrives or does not measure up to the description, there is really not much recourse, except to post negative feedback on eBay. In cases where sellers are so trusting that they send their merchandise before the payment clears, buyers bear the burden of proving that they are trustworthy. To prove themselves within the community, they must establish that they are trustworthy by buying several times. As soon as they have accumulated a high positive rating, they have also a higher chance to succeed as sellers.

Not many people would send a cheque for that amount of money to someone they did not know at all, based on a promise and a few emails

Returning to the example of the used laptop, the risk for the buyer in San Francisco is considerably lower if the seller already has a positive rating of 50 or more. Obviously, it is less risky to send $800 to someone with a record of 50 successful transactions than to someone you do not know at all. A favourable rating as a buyer can also benefit the same person as a seller. Let us say there are two absolutely identical laptops up for auction, one from a seller with a rating of zero and one from a seller with a positive rating of 200. Which one would you bid for? Since the buyer has to send the money first and then rely on the honesty of the seller, more people will bid for the laptop with the high seller rating. The rating becomes a measure of trust with a cash value within the eBay community, and there is little incentive for people with high ratings to exploit potential buyers.

The rating system seems to work very well for eBay since there are quite a few auctions with prices over $5,000 run on the site that would probably never take place without the rating system. Not many people would send a cheque for that amount of money to someone they did not know at all, based on a promise and a few emails.

The eBay rating functions well as a relative certification of trustworthiness, but it cannot be transferred to other web sites. If someone has a high rating, he cannot transfer the trust he has accumulated to another web site because there is no way to verify that he actually is the person he claims to be. Only eBay can identify the individual through his password.

Obviously, hardly anyone has a negative total rating on eBay because no one would do business with such a person. A wilful swindler can circumvent this protection by registering again under a new name and starting all over again. The company can identify someone by a single password but not someone who logs on under different names and passwords. The rating system is an incentive for the honest user to log on under the same name, of course, because otherwise he can never accumulate a high positive rating.

Only an absolute certification can make sure that laura@aol.com is actually Ms Laura Wintersley born on June 5, 1968, in Warwick, Rhode Island

Theoretically, a user could run auctions as both buyer and seller under different names, and create a high positive rating, which he could use to swindle other users. It takes a great deal of effort, however, to run and pay for 30 or 40 fake auctions with enough different email addresses just for the chance to defraud two or three people. The number could not be more than that because the negative comments on the web site would raise red flags to other users.

But the example shows that relative certification always has limitations and, in the long run, will only reach its full benefit if it can be combined with absolute certification. A relative certification will always mean that you still do not know who the other person is, only that it is a person with a particular rating. Only an absolute certification can make sure that laura@aol.com is actually Ms Laura Wintersley born on June 5, 1968, in Warwick, Rhode Island.

An interesting alternative might open up with the use of mobile telephones as Internet access terminals

An interesting alternative might open up with the use of mobile telephones as Internet access terminals. Internet access via mobile telephones makes it much easier to identify the customer, although, again, different people might use the same phone. But here you might even be able to obtain more information about the customer, because apart from recent buying patterns in different shops, you can also determine where exactly the customer is. So when you know from his previous buying patterns that he is in the process of furnishing an apartment and you know that he is just walking by an interior design shop you can prompt an advertisement of that shop.

Reputation

Identification of business partners works both ways, of course. Not only does the selling company want to know who a customer is, but the customer, whether an individual or a company, also wants to know with whom they are dealing. This is especially important on the Internet where you only see the web presence of a company and have no chance to judge the company by, say, the look and size of a physical plant, which might carry an aura of substance.

Corporations have considerable advantages over consumers in communicating trustworthiness on the Internet. A well-known corporation can use its brand name to communicate trust. Since it is always one party that bears the risk of an Internet transaction, which is the party that fulfils its side of the deal first, it is sufficient for only one partner to be trustworthy to make the transaction possible.

If a person wants to buy a computer online from Dell and must send payment first, he will be more willing to send a cheque than if it were some totally unfamiliar company, which might not even exist apart from the web site and has never sold a computer in the course of its existence. For many companies this option will also be limited to the country of origin because well known and reputable brand names in, say, Korea might be completely unheard of in France, for example.

Trusted third party

In order to exchange the product and the payment securely, there is also the possibility of using a trusted third party. This means that buyer and seller send money and the product to a third party who executes the transaction. What looks cumbersome at first sight is simpler than it appears. One option would be to send the goods via FedEx or UPS 'cash on delivery'. In this case the product and the money are in the same place at the same time. The buyer receives the product before he has to pay and the seller is sure to get the money through the intermediary.

Another possibility is a service such as I-Escrow (***www.iescrow.com***). This web site is used to facilitate the transaction if buyer and seller do not know each other and cannot come to the same place at the same time. Once the buyer and the seller have found each other on the Internet, through an online auction for example, they can decide to do the transaction via I-Escrow. They register at the site and inform I-Escrow about the transaction, the amount to be paid and the period of time that the buyer has to evaluate the product. The buyer then pays the full purchase amount to I-Escrow, plus a small fee.

I-Escrow informs the seller when the money has been paid and that he can go ahead and ship the product. When it arrives the buyer has a pre-determined time – at least one day – to evaluate it. If he does not object, the payment is transferred from I-Escrow to the seller. If he objects, he returns it and receives his money back as soon as the seller has received the product. So buyer and seller do not have to trust each other; they only have to trust the third party.

virtual visit

Identification as a basis for customization

Knowing who you are dealing with and that your business partner has a solid record of paying bills, and has the money available to pay, is good as far as it goes. This information does not help you much, however, if you want to customize your communication, products or prices to the individual needs and preferences of the customer.

> **Knowing who you are dealing with and that your business partner has a solid record of paying bills, and has the money available to pay, is good as far as it goes**

For customization you need information about the customer's needs and preferences. The more a customer buys from a given retailer and the more information the retailer has about that customer, the better the retailer can tailor the product offering to individual needs. There are two different ways for the retailer to obtain this information: by observing the customer's actions or asking him questions.

Point of entry

Without asking the customer any direct questions, Internet retailers can learn a great deal about him by looking at the links he used to enter the retailer's web site. This can be especially valuable if the point of entry is a web site that caters to people with particular interests. For example, if a customer enters a travel agent's web site through the site of a scuba diver community, this detail points the travel agent towards offerings on scuba-diving destinations.

> **Someone surfing the web from Rome using his employer's corporate network might be wrongly identified as someone from New York if the headquarters and Internet access point are in New York**

If the analysis shows that the customer lives in a wealthy area, this, too, could serve as a first indication of possible interests and needs. The retailer can also learn from knowing the entry point the customer logged on to the web, indicating the country and the region. This information is only a first indication and might not necessarily be useful. Someone surfing the web from Rome using his employer's corporate network might be wrongly identified as someone from New York if the headquarters and Internet access point are in New York.

Buying and surfing patterns

The web site can also obtain a wealth of information by analyzing buying and surfing patterns. A customer might buy a high percentage of luxury goods or always select the cheapest offering; he might buy diapers frequently, thus indicating that he has a baby; perhaps he has even booked a golf holiday through the retailer's web site last year.

The customer might click on certain explanations of terms on the web site thus identifying himself as a non-expert. If the database allows analysis of such data, surfing patterns can yield invaluable information. In addition to actual buying patterns, the retailer can analyze which products the customer has looked at without buying and at what level of detail he reviewed them. Firefly (**www.firefly.com**) offers software to support analysis of buying and surfing patterns and a tool to make recommendations based on purchases by other customers. Firefly also supports the exchange of customer information between its other client companies.

Questions to the customer

Of course, the easiest way to obtain information about customers is simply to ask. However, unless there is some immediate benefit, they might be reluctant to answer. Even if the retailer asks only one question, there should be an obvious benefit for the customer. For example, if an online grocer asks a customer if she is a vegetarian, there is an immediate benefit for the customer if the web site subsequently displays only vegetarian foods and offers vegetarian recipes when she logs on. Similarly, if a travel agent asks a customer about the sports he likes, there would be an immediate benefit if the web site shows him only hotels featuring those sports. Much of this information could also be obtained if the retailer tracks the customer's selections while surfing on the web site, but with more work and a higher error rate. Just because the web site offers the customer predominantly those things that are in line with the personal profile, does not mean that the customer cannot actively select other products or services. The vegetarian might want to buy meat for a barbecue with friends and the passionate diver might decide to go golfing this year. Of course, these options are available, but for people with certain profiles they are not displayed prominently.

If the retailer cannot deliver immediate customer benefits through tailored product offerings, he can always offer tangible benefits in return for answering questions

If the retailer cannot deliver immediate customer benefits through tailored product offerings, he can always offer tangible benefits in return for answering questions. Probably one of the most important pieces of information a retailer can get is a customer's email address. If the email address is not required to deliver the product itself, there are other ways to obtain it. The retailer could ask for the email address to confirm an order or to inform the customer about order status and expected delivery time; the retailer could ask the customer for his email address and, in return, offer free first-time delivery, a six-month warranty extension on ordered products or bonus points in the retailer's customer loyalty programme. Questions can also be asked in exchange for service. A web site that offers free downloads could ask you a question every time you download something for free. To make sure that customers are not put off, however, questions should be asked very selectively, and each time it should be clear how the customer will benefit.

> **If the retailer gives the customer the ability to tailor the web site to her needs, and the customer takes advantage of this feature, there is a high probability that the customer will identify herself to that web site next time around**

Taking another tack, the retailer could let the customer herself tailor the site to her own personal needs and preferences. The customer could, for example, remove the areas of the product range in which she has no interest, and select the ones in which she does. For instance, a romantic customer might want to be informed via email about every weekend flight special from her home city to Venice. If the retailer gives the customer the ability to tailor the web site to her needs, and the customer takes advantage of this feature, there is a high probability that the customer will identify herself to that web site next time around.

Value and use of identification

The information accumulated about the customer becomes more valuable as more information is added to the profile, but this is only possible if the retailer can identify the customer as being the same person when he comes to the web site the next time.

Currently the only way the retailer can identify the user without the conscious help of the user himself is with a 'cookie'. A cookie is a piece of digital information that is stored on the individual user's computer and identifies him, web sites he has been to and details of transactions, such as user IDs, passwords or the last page visited. When the person comes to the same web site again the server is able to read the cookie stored on the computer, thus identifying the person. It is important to note that this again is not an absolute identification but only a relative one. You still do not know in absolute terms everything about the customer, but you know that it is a guy who spent 35 minutes last Sunday afternoon searching your travel agent web site for charter specials from Houston, Texas, to Kingstown, Jamaica, for December 23. To you he is no longer Joe Bloggs about whom you know nothing at all but someone who may live in Texas and may want to spend his Christmas holidays in the Caribbean.

Unfortunately, cookies have several major drawbacks. Not every person active on the Internet uses one computer. Some people might use several computers to surf the web, one at home and one at work, for example. Others might share their computer with the whole family and everyone uses it to surf. People change jobs and the computer changes, too. People buy new hardware and the accumulated cookies are lost.

Combining all of these factors over several years could greatly complicate your ability to keep track of your customers or potential customers, severely limiting the usefulness of cookies. On top of all of these problems there are people who do not like the idea of cookies and make an extra effort to avoid being identified. Customers are increasingly concerned about online privacy and question the value of voluntarily abdicating their right to privacy. In many countries, legislation limits companies' ability to gather information without the customer's knowledge and permission. And again we find the phenomenon of a traditional government task now being provided by private institutions as well. There is software available to prevent the posting of cookies on the computer and in most browsers the user can select whether he wants to accept cookies or not. There is software available for surfing the web incognito, which makes it impossible to post a cookie or to trace back the point of entry. The key to overcoming this reluctance is to apprise privacy-conscious consumers that their information has value to them as well as to Internet vendors.

Unfortunately, cookies have several major drawbacks

When they begin to see tangible benefits to surrendering some element of privacy to your company, they may be more willing to cooperate.

Thus, cookies are a good start for relative identification of customers or potential customers, but for the long run you have to figure out a way to ensure that they will voluntarily identify themselves to you. The prerequisite for voluntary identification is instilling trust that your company will handle the collected data absolutely confidentially.

In many countries, legislation limits companies' ability to gather information without the customer's knowledge and permission

Most customers may not be too happy to see their names and addresses together with their recent buying patterns or surfing patterns being sold on to third parties. Depending on what they bought or where they have surfed, the information could prove embarrassing if it became publicly known. Witness the plight of a US Supreme Court nominee whose taste in X-rated movie rentals emerged in confirmation hearings. Customers, therefore, need to know – and deserve to know – what information is collected, what it is used for and, in particular, whether it is sold or given to third parties. Information that the customer has actively entered into his personal profile should always be available for him to see and modify, if necessary. The information that the retailer has collected by watching the surfing and buying patterns should obviously not be disclosed to third parties, but does not necessarily have to be disclosed to the customer either.

Transparency and confidentiality are only the bare minimum, however. By themselves they will not be sufficient to motivate most users to identify themselves. You need to have incentives as well, some tangible benefit for the customer. In order to customize the selling process, the retailer needs the information about the customer as quickly as possible when he enters the web site. One of the biggest incentives for a customer to identify himself immediately is a customized user interface. This could be personal and confidential account information in the case of an online bank. It could also be certain areas of the web site that are available only to registered users even though the registration might be available free of charge. And it could be areas of the web site that are only available to paying users.

> **Witness the plight of a US Supreme Court nominee whose taste in X-rated movie rentals emerged in confirmation hearings**

But there are also incentive possibilities for identification even if you are not handling confidential information, charging for use or requiring registration. One option is to customize the communication interface. If someone regularly shops at an online supermarket, he probably has certain foods that he buys over and over again. Instead of having to search through the whole online store each time, the user would see his personal shopping list each time he identifies himself, and he only has to select the quantities of these items that he wants to buy that week. The tangible incentive for thus identifying himself is this ability to take advantage of the personalized interface.

If you still cannot convince the customer to identify himself when he enters the web site, there should at least be some incentive to make sure that he identifies himself once he has decided to buy. For the second purchase, for example, he should not have to key in his address, credit card numbers or other vital information; for subsequent purchases, only his name and password would be required. The added convenience is an incentive to identify himself. If a web site offers a bonus programme for loyal customers, the customer also has an incentive to identify himself in order to accumulate bonus points.

While it is usually easy to design mechanisms that will induce the customer to identify himself once he wants to buy something, it is much more difficult to design incentives for the customer to identify himself as soon as he enters the web site. Obviously, identification at the beginning is much more valuable for the retailer because he can use current shopping time to communicate with the customer based on needs and preferences, thus increasing the chance of an eventual sale.

One of the biggest incentives for a customer to identify himself immediately is a customized user interface

Chapter 8

Information about product features

In the last chapter we discussed the different options for identifying business partners as a basis for transactions and also as a basis for customization. As we have shown, uncertainty about who you are buying from or selling to can inhibit trade because you need to trust that the counterparty will fulfil his share of the deal.

In addition to information about your business partner, however, you also have to be able to communicate the features of the product or service that you want to sell. People want to know what they are getting before they spend their money on it.

It used to be common wisdom that the Internet could only be used for the sale of standardized, easily transportable goods such as books or CDs and had no value for perishables or big-ticket items like cars. Most of these assumptions have already been proven to be untrue; witness the rise of online supermarkets and auto dealers whose success has excited the imaginations of almost every conceivable kind of manufacturer. Some products, however, *are* easier to market than others. Communicating product features via the Internet is not necessarily easy and requires a good deal of thought, especially when you think about customizing your product or service.

> **It used to be common wisdom that the Internet could only be used for the sale of standardized, easily transportable goods such as books or CDs and had no value for perishables or big-ticket items like cars**

The easiest way to sell over the Internet is to sell something the buyer is already familiar with. This is often the case in the business-to-business trade, where the same product is bought many times over from the same supplier. Even products that require a lot of initial sales effort the first time can be sold through the web for repeat buys, so one option might be to make the first sale through your traditional sales channels, but do repeat business of the same product through the Internet.

If your primary sales channel is your own sales team, an Internet strategy will ultimately compel you to rethink how it is deployed. You might be able to reduce the size of the sales force as repeat selling depends less and less on sales calls. Better, however, would be to refocus team activity on winning new key accounts.

> **Refocus team activity on winning new key accounts**

If your primary sales channel lies outside your own company, you will most likely run into a channel conflict. The retailer who has been selling your products will probably not be too keen on losing most of his repeat business, which is usually very profitable for him because the customer needs less attention the second time around – the same reason that probably makes it ideal for the Internet. These resellers might actually have the power to prevent the manufacturer from selling online in the short run by threatening to stop selling the products of this particular manufacturer, something the manufacturers may not be able to afford. Severe channel conflicts can keep a manufacturer from entering the online world.

The short-term danger of alienating existing sales channels, however, can lead to long-term disaster. New competitors can enter the market, building their online sales capability from scratch. This is the real test. If the retailer adds no value and can be replaced by the Internet, his fate is inevitable. The only question is whether the manufacturer manages to pull together an online presence in time or whether he will vanish from the marketplace together with his retailers. Companies which manage to redefine their distribution to ensure that each party involved adds value to the process will succeed. Those companies that manage to solve their value-chain conflicts first are most likely to be the winners in the future.

The short-term danger of alienating existing sales channels can lead to long term disaster

There is no mistaking the larger trend. It is the nature of the web as a communication medium that it will render superfluous many of today's retailers and intermediaries, no matter how long they have survived. Products that have well-known brand names have no problem communicating the product features via the Internet. Everybody knows them anyway and has used them before. With these products, retailers and other intermediaries create little value because they have nothing to add to the product story that cannot be told more cheaply and efficiently over the Internet.

The same is true for many repeat buys or spare part orders. In this case, communication of the product features is not an issue. The customer probably knows little about the product and does not want to know. He just knows that he needs to find a certain spare part for a specific device, which can be a pretty nerve-racking process. Not all dealers stock all spare parts for every product they sell; it would be much too expensive. So the customer is faced with the choice of calling one dealer after the other until he finally finds the desired spare part or ordering it through the dealer. Most customers, particularly small businesses, do not have the habit of stocking spare parts, which puts them under considerable pressure when something breaks, because they cannot use the device until they get the part. The quicker they can get it, the better.

Those companies that manage to solve their value-chain conflicts first are most likely to be the winners in the future

The Internet offers added convenience if the customer can order the desired part for prompt delivery directly from the original manufacturer, or from someone who specializes in distributing spare parts for different manufacturers.

The Internet also offers a specially good opportunity for value-added services for spare parts if the customer only knows that the whole device does not work any more but has no idea what particular part needs replacing. A detailed online troubleshooting and analysis guide can help the customer identify the broken part by himself and then order it without replacing the whole thing.

Airline tickets are another example of the kind of item that can be easily sold via the Internet. Again this is a commonly known product. The web can communicate all necessary information about a British Airways flight from London to San Francisco: departure time, arrival time, number of intermediate stops, flight price for the selected class and date, seat availability, leg room between seats in the selected class, title of in-flight movie, food service and on and on – already more information than most travel agents can offer their customers. The different components of the service can actually be communicated better via the web than through a travel agent or airline representative.

These are examples of products whose characteristics are clearly defined or already known to the customer. But what do you do if your product or service is not commonly known? In such cases you have to rely on the web to communicate the product features.

Digitized product features

Any product or service information that can be digitized can be communicated through the Internet – written text, pictures and videos or music. Thus, your customer can look at a picture of, say, a computer and read the detailed product description; she can compare interest rates at different banks; she can see a picture of a book cover and read the first chapter; she can see clips of a pop group performance before buying a CD or video. Some products themselves can be digitized: books, newspapers, music, games and software could be completely communicated via the web.

> **Any product or service information that can be digitized can be communicated through the Internet**

This full product delivery capability for digitized information creates problems of its own. One party to the transaction – manufacturer or customer – has to trust the other to fulfil his share of the bargain. In a traditional store, a customer could return the product for cash or store credit. With Internet-borne information products, the customer actually does not know if the product is worth the price until he has seen the whole thing. The manufacturer, for his part, has to charge the whole price up front because otherwise he might never get paid.

There are several ways to resolve this conflict. The most common solution is to communicate only part of the product via the web, as in the example of the first chapter of a book, or in the case of the first track from the new Madonna CD. This could be the preferred option if you sell items where one is very different from the other, such as books and CDs. However, it makes no sense if you are trying to sell two different authors or artists. There is no point in giving the entire Madonna CD for free on the assumption that you will make it up later when the customer pays for a Mariah Carey CD. Just because your customer likes Madonna is no guarantee that she will also like Mariah Carey.

If you are selling products of consistent quality but they depend for their value on constantly changing content, the situation is different. You can give away the *Wall Street Journal* online for a limited period of time, and thus communicate all the paper's features. But because the customer cannot continue to rely on the same few issues indefinitely, the customer has every incentive to pay for it if he likes it.

Certification by third parties

In the event that the product is difficult or impossible to digitize, you need to find other ways to communicate product features. One is certification by third parties. This is a common procedure in buying art – most collectors must rely on experts to certify the authenticity of Old Master paintings, for example.

When Consumer Reports (**www.consumerreports.org**) in the USA or Stiftung Warentest (**www.warentest.de**) in Germany certify that a dishwasher is among the best of its class, there is no need to go to the store and look at it. Here the opinion of the expert is even better than looking at the product itself. Of course, to recognize a good dishwasher you don't have to be an expert. You just put the dirty dishes inside, turn the machine on and check if the dishes are clean afterwards. Unfortunately, stores usually do not let you bring your dirty dishes in for a 'test wash'.

Unfortunately, stores do not usually let you bring your dirty dishes in for a 'test wash'

Therefore, even when you go to the store, you have to rely on the opinion of recognized experts who have actually tested the machines. Although the actual product features of a dishwasher are difficult to convey digitally, the result of the certification can be communicated very well via the web. Sellers can link their web sites to others maintained by qualified experts to save the customer the trouble of finding them, instead of reprinting favourable reviews within the vendor's proprietary site. This kind of linkage is a good compromise. The integrity of the evaluation is itself certified by the arm's length linkage.

If there are no expert certifications because the nature of the product does not lend itself to such review, the comments of other users can serve as 'expert' opinion, especially if product quality is a subjective matter. The key is for users to give enough information to allow the potential customer to make a thoughtful evaluation – stars or thumbs up are not really enough.

virtual visits

Displaying both good and bad customer feedback on the web site gives the retailer credibility, which is extremely important in the impersonal Internet environment

Displaying both good and bad customer feedback on the web site gives the retailer credibility, which is extremely important in the impersonal Internet environment. For example, Amazon is not afraid of displaying negative comments about its books; every comment is always couched as a reader's personal opinion. The more customer feedback there is, the easier it is for a new customer to make an informed decision. If a travel agent's web site displays a 'negative' customer comment because a hotel has no discotheque, someone else may choose the same hotel for that very reason. The examples show that user-generated content can serve to communicate product or service features and may in many cases be more helpful or more credible than the description provided by the seller himself.

Brand reputation

If you have looked at all the possibilities of communicating product features via the web and you have concluded that they do not work for your business, that is no reason to despair. The problem is not unique to the Internet. Plenty of firms out there in the bricks and mortar world find it very hard to communicate their product or service features, and yet they still do good business.

Take management consulting as an example. If a corporation decides that it wants to establish its online presence with the help of a management consulting company, it basically has thousands to choose from. Some will do a good job, others will not perform so well. Still, it is very important to get it right the first time because the market is not likely to give you a second chance. So choosing the right consultant is crucial.

It is very important to get it right the first time because the market is not likely to give you a second chance

The product in management consulting is by definition customized, and on top of that it is highly confidential; the consulting companies will usually not show their previous 'products' to potential clients. Therefore, they rely heavily on brand reputation. Instead of judging the individual product, the buyer relies on the fact that the selected well-known company always delivers high-quality results. This brand reputation makes up for the fact that the actual product or service features cannot be communicated at the time the contract is closed.

To build a solid brand reputation or transfer the brand reputation that you already have from the bricks and mortar world to the virtual world is a very efficient way to get around the problem of communicating product features. A solid brand reputation allows you to sell even perishables via the web. Admittedly it can be difficult to communicate online whether the Granny Smith apples you are selling are actually fresh and ripe. But if you have a reputation for selling only high-quality groceries, and if your customers are pleased with your merchandise, it should not be a problem selling perishables to them via the web as well. The brand reputation works both ways, however. If you send spoiled goods to your customer once, you are not likely to be required to send a **further order.**

Mail sample

It is easy to communicate most features of most products via the Internet, but there remain a few things that just cannot be communicated very well digitally. Suppose you are trying to sell custom-made shirts. It is possible to communicate the size of the shirt, the form of the collar and the cuffs and the length of the arms digitally. It starts getting difficult when your customer is trying to figure out if the blue fabric he has selected will actually go with the grey suit hanging in his wardrobe.

One possibility is to send a sample of the fabric to the customer before he buys the shirt. The customer gets the chance to select from a real fabric sample and determine all the other features digitally.

Another option is to give away the first product free so the user gets to know the product features. This makes sense only under two conditions: first, if the user can be definitively identified, because otherwise the same user would sign up under different names and you would never get paid. Second, if the business relies on repeat buys and the marginal costs of one product are close to zero. This is especially the case, as stated earlier, for all information products that are delivered directly through the web or by mail on CD-ROM. If you have an extensive library of digital photos that you want to market online to graphic designers and commercial artists, you can always mail one for free so they see the quality for themselves. Here, even without being able to identify your customer you can prevent abuse by always using the same picture when a sample is requested.

> **Another option is to give away the first product free so the user gets to know the product features**

Right to return goods ....

To ease customer uncertainty about the features of the selected product further the company can offer a return option. Dell Computers, for example, takes back all its machines within 30 days with no questions asked. This is noteworthy since the product features of a computer can be communicated digitally very well and there is fundamentally no customer uncertainty about the product features, apart from the question of whether the computer will work at all. Dell will not only take back computers that are 'dead on arrival' but any computer the customer does not like for whatever reason. This is especially remarkable since all Dell computers are built to order for the particular customer and cannot be resold for the full price to another customer.

There are various ways to communicate product features via the Internet, which can, in fact, be used in combination to reinforce each other

Nevertheless, Dell feels that the return option is very important for its business. Dell was already offering a 30-day return option for its computers before it started selling on the Internet because it has always sold PCs directly to the customer, with no chance for buyers to look at the product before purchase. Since Dell sells primarily to corporate accounts, however, the chance that the option will be abused is not very high.

Mail order businesses are another example of companies that use return options extensively to overcome the problem of communicating product features, and are an obvious model for Internet sales. Mail order catalogues create a large part of their revenue through the sale of clothing and shoes. The security afforded to the customer by a return policy seems to overcome the uncertainty about the product features, such as the actual fit of garments.

The return option only makes sense both for buyer and seller, however, if it is actually possible to specify the product via the Internet. If the sale of a product needs face-to-face interaction of buyer and seller because the buyer has very refined specifications and the seller has to contribute specific know-how and consulting services, it will be difficult to conclude the whole sale via the web. It is, theoretically, also possible to buy a nuclear power plant via the Internet but it would be a rather tedious process. The option of returning the power plant free of charge would not really be of much help, apart from the tremendous cost of such an offer.

The tools in this section show that there are various ways to communicate product features via the Internet, which can, in fact, be used in combination to reinforce each other. Even if you come to the conclusion that in your particular industry the Internet cannot communicate all the features of your product adequately, the Internet might still change the way you sell it.

Take cars, for example. In the bricks and mortar world, a car dealer has three functions. He will explain all the features and special equipment of the car to you, show you the car or let you test drive it, and third, possibly arrange financing. Now, explanation of the car's functionality, special equipment, possible combination of features, and pricing and the approval of a loan can all be done via the Internet. But no matter how sophisticated your web site, it will be difficult to convey the feeling of what it is like actually to sit in the new car and drive it.

What is different now, however, is that the buyer does not necessarily need a qualified dealer any more. He just needs someone who hands over the car for a test drive. The possibility of separating the task of providing test drives from the task of explaining the car to the customer offers a whole new range of opportunities for selling cars.

For the manufacturer this offers alternatives to the sales channel 'car dealer'. Partnerships with car rental companies, where the potential customer might drive the car for a day for a reduced rate, or taxis, where people can order a ride in the desired car, could be an alternative to keeping an expensive network of retailers. If the business traveller who often rents cars or rides in taxis is the target group for buying a new car, it might be an interesting possibility.

Very few products can be imagined where the Internet does not at least change the selling process

Currently car sale through the Internet is not really difficult, because people can always go to a car dealer and have a look at the car or even test drive it and order it on the Internet later. This model is not sustainable in the long run, however, because car dealers would not make any money any more and would close down. And car dealers would heavily object if the same car were sold for a lower price on the Internet, because the customer would presumably test drive it at the dealer and later buy it for the lower price via the web.

All in all, there will always remain some product features that cannot be adequately communicated through the web. However, by employing the models described here, very few products can be imagined where the Internet does not at least change the selling process. So far we have focused on communicating product features via the web. Clearly, there are a number of ways of accomplishing this, and there are several tools that can make up for features that cannot be communicated very well on the web, although in some cases they are decidedly inferior to a visit to a bricks and mortar business. However, in later chapters we will show additional electronic commerce possibilities for customization of communication, product and price that could never be imagined in the bricks and mortar world.

Part IV

Customized communication

Chapter 9

Cutomization models

Imagine, if you will, the golden age of consumer retailing. The owner of the corner greengrocery has known you since you had to hold your mother's hand when you walked on the street. As you walk in the door he greets you by name, asks you about your family and says he has some of those Spanish oranges that were such a treat when you were a child. Then you go to the fishmonger who remembers your weakness for wild salmon and informs you that he has some fresh from an estate in Scotland. At the clothing shop where you used to buy your knee socks for school they have that blouse in just your colour. And so on down the high street: each shopkeeper is friendly and attentive with your taste and price range in his head.

Coming back to the world of today, we realize that for the most part in these days of anonymous hypermarkets and big-box discounters, this kind of personal shopping experience has been lost. Personal relationships with retailers are exceptions. Retailers cannot tailor offers to specific customers and their needs any more.

> **Personal relationships with retailers are exceptions. Retailers cannot tailor offers to specific customers and their needs any more**

Instead of personal relationships, retailers reach out through advertising. In theory, retailers could use information about customers' individual needs and preferences if they could only make connections between particular customers and related products. If there are heavy sales of diapers in a supermarket one week, it is highly likely that those buyers will be interested in a special offer for baby food the next. But because the retailer cannot attribute diaper purchases to any specific shoppers, he advertises a special on baby food in the local newspaper, even though at least 90 per cent of the people who read the ad will buy no baby food, regardless of the price or the amount of advertising. Why not? No baby!

Online sales can be a retailer's dream come true. Because of the wealth of information that can be digitized, retailers can tailor the communication about products or services to specific customers' needs. There are two basic models that can be used for customization, active customization, initiated by the customer, and passive customization, initiated by the retailer or manufacturer. Most of the time both models are used in combination, to allow for maximum coverage. The two models will be used throughout the rest of the book and can be applied to the customization of pricing and production as well as communication.

Active customization

> **Active customization means that the customer initiates the request for customized emails or information on the web site, which will then appear whenever the retailer has something to offer**

Active customization means that the customer initiates the request for customized emails or information on the web site, which will then appear whenever the retailer has something to offer. Active customization requires no prior information about the customer, because the customer volunteers it. An example would be a customer who actively selects certain categories of an online newspaper that he would like to read and also requests email notifications for certain events that are of special interest to him.

Active customization can result in a communication pattern, product or service that is actually unique to one customer. A travel agent could offer customized email notification if prices to pre-selected destinations drop below a certain level and seats are available on specific days. A customer living in Singapore could ask to be notified by email every time the price for a flight from Singapore to Bali drops below $400 with selected airlines and there are seats available for two people to fly there Friday night after 6 pm and come back Monday morning before 9 am. A stock broker can notify the customer each time the price for a certain stock falls below a pre-determined level while the stock index is above a certain level.

The cost of a single email is almost identical to that for multiple emails once the underlying computer system is set up

The customer must stay within the limits of the options that the web site offers, naturally, but apart from that the resulting communication can actually be individualized. It may be that no one else in the world is interested in that specific bit of information. Therefore if the criteria selected by the customer apply, the web site would send exactly one email and no more. This is still economically feasible because the cost of a single email is almost identical to that for multiple emails once the underlying computer system is set up. The costly part, which is inputting the information, is done by the customer.

Active customization also allows the retailer to collect valuable information about customers' needs and preferences, which he can use to tailor offerings further. He can also aggregate the information on a higher level and sell it to manufacturers. A list of 10,000 customers who have asked to be notified if a certain product is available for a specific price could be very valuable to manufacturers, especially if they receive exclusive rights to it.

If the manufacturer decides to produce the product according to the articulated needs of the customers, during a time of low capacity utilization, everyone could profit

If the manufacturer decides to produce the product according to the articulated needs of the customers, during a time of low capacity utilization, for example, everyone could profit. Customers would be informed that the product they were looking for is available for the desired price. The owner of the web site would receive a commission on sales and thus increase his revenue. The manufacturer could fully utilize capacity and simultaneously increase his revenue.

Passive customization

Passive customization means that the retailer uses the information he has about the customer to tailor the communication to the customer's likely needs. An example would be a customer who booked a diving holiday last year and has searched the travel agent's web site for this year's Christmas diving specials. The customer could now be notified by email that someone else has cancelled a reservation and that airline seats and hotel reservations for the desired destination and travel time are available. In this case the customer has only surfed the web site, but has not actively requested specific information. Nevertheless the passive customized communication is tailored to his needs. The customer does not necessarily know that a customization has taken place. He might think that the holiday mail is just a regular mailing directed at thousands of people that just happens to fit his personal preferences very well.

To initiate passive customization, the retailer programs the computer with a set of criteria. When those criteria are fulfilled, the computer acts. Passive customization is usually done for the large groups necessary to justify defining the selection criteria. However, if the web site selects the options by matching buying patterns of individuals, passive customization could also result in a unique offering.

Both active and passive customization can be done on two levels. First, the communication and customer interface can be customized on a broad level for a distinct group of customers, and then they can be customized on a more individual level. Take the example of a company using the web to sell computers to corporate customers. On the first level of customization, the company can design a special web site that can be incorporated into the Intranets of its key clients, each with a unique look, incorporating the client's company logo and the look and feel of the client's Intranet. Then, on the content side, a business customer could require that all of the computers would have a monitor from a certain manufacturer, but must be bought without disk drives in order to protect the company's computer network from viruses. Therefore, the customized web site would offer monitors only from that single manufacturer and would not carry any disk drives at all. It could even include specifications for different uses within the company. For example, the graphics department and the finance department would have different standard specifications.

> **If the web site selects the options by matching buying patterns of individuals, passive customization could also result in a unique offering**

Such a web site is the first level of customization. The second level would be the customization done by a client's employee who orders a particular computer for his department. The next time this employee returns to the web site, it could already be primed with the details of the computer he bought last time, the delivery address and the internal charge number. Therefore, he does not have to go through the whole selection process again but can save time by making only a few changes to his last order. The customization for the company could even go further and include features of client work flow systems. Apart from prompting for an appropriate charge number for the client's accounting systems, it could also automatically forward the order to the person in charge of approving the order and route the bill to the finance department.

On most web sites where the seamless flow of information is crucial, we find relatively high set-up costs and greatly reduced running costs

Thus, customized web sites can be totally integrated into the computer and work flow systems of the customer. The initial costs to set up such a customized web site are relatively high. However, the cost of the individual transaction is extremely low. The computer manufacturer saves manpower in sales, order entry, and customer care. The client company saves costs on purchasing department personnel and internal red tape.

On most web sites where the seamless flow of information is crucial, we find relatively high set-up costs and greatly reduced running costs. This cost structure almost inevitably gives the first mover a big advantage over latecomers. Once one computer company has managed to integrate its systems into the client's Intranet, the chances for a second or third supplier to participate significantly are rather slim.

The more often the customer comes back the greater the possibilities for the retailer to obtain a more complete picture

As already described, digitized information can be analyzed quickly and cheaply and can therefore be used to generate more customized communication. Continuous access to current transaction data offers the possibility of closely monitoring customer behaviour on a day to day basis. The retailer can quickly build a learning relationship with the customer. Every time the customer visits the web site or buys something the retailer can analyze his behaviour and add to his overall knowledge of the customer. The more often the customer comes back the greater the possibilities for the retailer to obtain a more complete picture.

There are two levels to a learning relationship. First the retailer has to learn about the current wants and needs of the customer. From knowledge concerning a single product, a company can also take educated guesses about tastes and needs in other product categories and make suggestions accordingly.

The other level of the learning relationship is to find out or even anticipate how the customer's needs might change. Needs and tastes generally change over time. They especially tend to change with certain events, such as starting a first job, marriage, buying a house, moving to a different town or having a child. If your customer is a university student, her buying patterns will probably change significantly once she has her degree and starts to earn money.

Chapter 10

Meaningful communication

In bygone days, retail communication with the customer was always customized because it was, basically, one to one. With the advent of advertising and later mass mailing, companies used a scatter gun, knowing full well that sales would be a single-digit percentage of those who received the information, but that the few sales still made the mailing worthwhile.

As more companies started to communicate that way, however, the returns diminished. In a business model based on communication with end customers, the limiting factor is

> **In bygone days, retail communication with the customer was always customized because it was, basically, one to one**

no longer scarce resources or limited capital but the attention of the user. The more 'junk' mail arrives at the customer's home, the more gets thrown out unopened. The same pattern is emerging for the Internet.

In a business model based on communication with end customers, the limiting factor is no longer scarce resources or limited capital but the attention of the user

Currently, users have to be willing to search through immense amounts of information in order to find what they are looking for. Once customized communication becomes the norm, however, users will turn to web sites where offerings are tailored to their needs, either because they have built individual profiles or because there are enough people like them to justify those sites. Whether the company has a very focused target group and treats everyone the same, or has a very wide target group and customizes within that group, makes no difference to the customer, who only sees the end result. It makes a huge difference for the company, however, because a much larger target customer group can allow it to leverage the costs of web sites, production plants and distribution systems.

Customized communication always has to be meaningful for the recipient. If the user sees no value in the information he receives, it might be 'customized' in the sense that it is being sent to a small number of people, but it is completely wasted. Customized communication increases the convenience for the user because it delivers pre-selected information that is adapted to the user's preferences. This can be done through customized mailings and a customized user interface. Customized mailings inform the user about specific areas of interest to him and are therefore means to increase the traffic on a web site. Customized user interfaces welcome the user with a web site interface that is adapted to his needs and therefore are means to increase the loyalty of the customer. The two means of communication are outlined in the following sections.

Customized user interface

In order to customize you need information about the person you want to cater for. Like a dress-maker who cannot start to tailor the dress without measuring the customer, you cannot start to tailor your user interface without information about the individual at the other end of the computer.

In an earlier chapter, we discussed various ways of obtaining information about the customer: point of entry and buying and surfing patterns were the basis for passive customization; direct questioning was outlined as the basis for active customization. Whether you use passive or active customization, however, the options presented are pretty much the same. Take the choice of language for doing business, for example. Let us say one of the options of the web site is a display of the content in different languages. With passive customization the server would choose the language according to the country where the customer comes from or the language of the previous web site she looked at. For active customization, the customer would select the preferred language on your homepage. Active and passive customization can both be used to customize other options on the web site and therefore support and complement one another.

> **Like a dressmaker who cannot start to tailor the dress without measuring the customer, you cannot start to tailor your user interface without information about the individual at the other end of the computer**

Active customization is the preferred option, of course, because when the customer participates, you can be sure that you have actually offered what he wants. If you conclude from the fact that the customer has logged on to the web in the USA and the last web site he looked at was in English that he prefers to see information displayed in English, you could be wrong. He might also be a Frenchman who logged on through the network of his international employer and only viewed the last web site in English because it was not available in French. If he selects French as his preferred language, however, then there is no doubt about his preference.

Companies from the USA, in particular, tend to think that everyone in the world speaks English anyway and are therefore content to present the web site only in English. Even if customers speak English, and are willing to buy in English in the absence of other options, it might not be their first choice. As long as you have a monopoly on the Internet you might well sell in English. But in a monopoly situation you can basically do anything anyway. You do not have to make any concessions to the customer concerning product features, price or language. In a free market economy, however, where the next competitor is just one click away, you might find that a lot of people who speak English will much prefer to buy in their own language. To insist on English will start to cost you the customers you have, never mind the ones you never made because they didn't understand your 'English only' web site in the first place.

> **Even if customers speak English, and are willing to buy in English in the absence of other options, it might not be their first choice**

The strategy that most Internet companies seem to follow currently is to begin with English and add other languages as the business grows. They are basically testing the product and the business concept in the very large and wealthy test market of the English-speaking population.

But the Internet itself is by definition global. And most products that are sold via the web today can be sold globally without much additional effort. UPS or Federal Express don't care if you want to ship to New York or Paris, because they operate globally anyway. For most products sold on the web today the language barrier is the biggest obstacle; books would be an exception because they are one of the few language-specific products.

For most products sold on the web today the language barrier is the biggest obstacle

The good news is that the language barrier on the Internet is easier to overcome than the language barrier in the bricks and mortar world. Your customers from France are not asking you to converse with them over the telephone in French or to write to them in French. The only thing they are asking for is a French-language web site. The web has made it simple to go global. A monolingual web site means giving up a chance fully to exploit the first mover advantage. Let us say you have decided to test your web business in the English-speaking market. Now imagine that your business really takes off; you are about to become another Amazon. But other companies are watching. When you have proved that your business model actually works, they quickly imitate it in other languages. You have English – they have everything else. By the time you get around to translating your web site, the competitor might already have built a brand reputation in his country and gained a large share of the market. Suddenly, you look like the imitator. What did you gain by testing your concept only in English? You became a very generous prototype for entrepreneurs around the world.

What did you gain by testing your concept only in English? You became a very generous prototype for entrepreneurs around the globe

The language in which you communicate is one of the most important elements of customization. If this first step fails, all other customization efforts will probably be in vain because potential customers have already left the site, frustrated by the language barrier, never to return. However, if you have given them a choice, you readily create goodwill that may pay off in the form of willingness to volunteer other information.

After you have determined the preferred language, the next important thing is to find out about the level of information the potential customer is expecting to find on the web site. Is this an expert or a beginner? For an expert you might want to display your information on a high level of detail, whereas a beginner might need more explanation of specific terms and expressions. The user of the web site is unlikely to identify herself as an expert or beginner by answering that question on the homepage, however. But she might very quickly identify herself through her surfing patterns. There are software programs such as ***www.personify.com*** that allow analysis of a browser's behaviour in real time, customization of the web site and identification of cross-selling opportunities.

Imagine that you have a web site on which you sell computers that are built to order for each individual customer. The way each customer acts while he configures the computer should quickly give you information about the customer himself. Someone who first clicks for a definition of CD-ROM is likely to be a beginner, whereas one who quickly selects the basic configurations and then dives into the details of different modem cards and configurations is more likely to be an expert.

For an expert, you might want to display your information on a high level of detail, whereas a beginner might need more explanation of specific terms and expressions … A virtual sales assistant might leap into action

Both users, basically, want to buy a computer. Nevertheless they have very different needs and you might gain by displaying information in different formats. While you still basically offer the same product options for both types of users, the presentation of the information might be different. The non-expert might be overwhelmed by excessive detail and give up before he finds what he needs. He might sign off and go to a computer store to buy a standard computer, blissfully ignorant of the inner workings of the computer and options that would have made his life better.

Just because you offer thousands of different choices on your web site does not mean you must display them prominently for every single user. Once you have determined by the first few clicks that the user knows very little you can adapt the communication of the information to his needs. The web site would then react like a good salesperson if he sees that the customer does not know very much about the product. Computer jargon would be eliminated. A virtual sales assistant might leap into action. Instead of asking whether the customer wanted a particular type of CD-ROM or processor type, it would ask how he wanted to use the computer and what kind of budget he had in mind. The virtual sales assistant would then configure a computer that met the customer's requirements. It would explain why it included the different features and what they can be used for. The virtual sales assistant could also suggest some additional features that would make sense for the user but had not been included because of budget limitations. The user can then accept the recommendation or change it. The huge advantage for the novice user is starting out with a machine that already matches most of his needs. He can then add or delete a few features.

The same virtual sales assistant that proved so helpful for the computer novice might be perceived as a personal insult by the expert. The expert knows exactly what she wants and shops for the exact product features and the lowest price. She might be looking for a specific modem card that is usually hard to find or she might need special network solutions. There is no need to limit the number of options for the expert or to avoid computer jargon. On the contrary, she would probably not take the web site seriously if a virtual sales assistant tried to explain the different options in plain English. Therefore, if you are designing the communication interface for the expert, the selling proposition you would try to communicate would be that the customer could find every exotic piece of equipment she could think of and build a computer with any combination of those pieces. This same message would scare the novice away.

Users should also always have an active choice between novice and expert levels of communication, or anything in between, at any point in the negotiation. Going from the novice level to a more sophisticated level should be just a key stroke away. Active customization by the user should always override any passive customization by the company. It would be commercially disastrous to impose a choice on the customer.

There are other communication considerations that are not related to the customer's level of sophistication but depend on individual preferences. When someone wants to buy a flat from a real estate agent, the Internet can take you only so far. Most people will not spend a few hundred thousand dollars without ever looking at the property themselves. But if a web site can narrow down the number of properties the buyer might want to look at, the web site can gain powerful competitive advantage over less convenient realtors.

Active customization by the user should always override any passive customization by the company.

The appeal of any house depends on a variety of things – location, look, floor plan, view and price, to name but a few. A real estate agent might provide a web site where all of these factors can be tested or looked at. But because different people have different priorities, these factors might be examined in the prospect's order of preference. One might first like to narrow down the school district and the price range. Another might not care about schools, but might have a dream of a particular kind of view that a locale is famous for.

After he has selected all the houses that meet his primary criterion, he might then start to consider secondary ones. If the web site offers the option to search only by zip code and then lists all offerings by price, the process of selecting a promising house via the Internet can become very tedious. This can be particularly burdensome if a family is relocating from another region or country. What this customer really needs is an option that says: 'Show me pictures of all houses with spectacular ocean views in a particular town.' This requires, of course, that the information is not only digitized but can be analyzed under those criteria, so when the house is entered into the web site, it is not enough to provide a picture with the view from the house, but it has also to be quantified if this is a bad, average or good ocean view. Cross-indexing with a limited price ceiling might eliminate some of the better ones, of course. The house shopper might quickly have to say goodbye to some of his dreams, but it would save him time.

Many real estate web sites assume that people select their house primarily according to location, size and price, and those are usually the only criteria that are analyzed for digitization. If your disqualifying criterion is whether the house has at least two separate bathrooms, you are faced again with the task of going through all the individual listings and checking. You have not really benefited very much compared to going through newspaper listings.

In fact, most real estate web sites are really just glorified classified ads, organized by location and price. Since print is not an interactive medium, it has had to live with listing by the one or two criteria presumed most important for most people. Customized listings allow every user to search according to his own priorities.

Customized listings allow every user to search according to his own priorities

In the same way that specialized web sites take over the function of classified ads in the newspaper, other web sites can also take over the function of the news and editorial pages. Just as the newspaper presents all houses for all readers, it presents the same articles to all readers, even though almost no one reads them all. But each reader reads a different fraction and the newspaper has no idea which ones read which fraction. The challenge for journalists and editors is to select the information each day that they think will most interest their clientele. For this model to work two prerequisites must be met: first, the readers of the paper have to have similar interests; second, the journalists and editors have to pick those things that will appeal to that particular group. Only those papers and magazines that manage both will flourish.

In the online world the rules of the game change considerably. First of all it is no longer crucial to serve a representative group of customers with one edition. Since the online newspaper can be adjusted to the interests of each individual reader it can serve much broader interests than a printed paper ever could. Both papers basically build on the same sources of information, but the printed paper is severely limited by the number of pages and therefore has to make a strict selection of the articles to be printed. They could, of course, increase the number of pages in the paper, but few people would want to have an encyclopedia delivered to their doorstep every morning, never mind the price. The value added in the printed paper lies in the pre-selection of information for a certain target group and a paper with several thousand pages would reduce that to absurdity. And the only help that the reader gets in selecting the articles that are of interest to him is in which section of the paper they are printed and what the headlines are.

Online newspapers, however, have a distinct advantage. Since they can deliver a different paper to every single customer they can rely on the power of customization. Both active and passive customization play an important role here. The paper can offer active customization options where the prospective reader specifies criteria and options that are of interest to him. From the sports section he might select to see all news about Manchester United; for politics he wants to see only the most important highlights; the arts pages he might not want to get at all and from the business section he selects the highlights and also every single piece of information about companies in which he owns shares.

The active customization is a good starting point in the case of online papers but in combination with passive customization the customer service can even go further. For passive customization, the publisher has to find out which articles the reader has actually read. There are several ways to do this. First, the user can be asked to fill in a questionnaire indicating the articles he liked. In a new relationship the user might get a questionnaire every week, whereas later in the learning curve he would only get one every one or two months.

Online newspapers have a distinct advantage. Since they can deliver a different paper to every single customer they can rely on the power of customization

Another possibility is to ask the user at the end of each article whether this information was useful or interesting for her or not. The user has to click once at the end of each article to get to the next article anyway and that click could simultaneously be used for feedback. The reader could have a red and a green button to exit the page and which one she uses would indicate whether she liked the article or not. All these options are actually just more sophisticated methods for active customization and a continuation of the initial questions posed to the new user.

The other option is to monitor, with the user's consent, which articles the user has read. If he reads his personal paper online, it is fairly easy for the web site to record which articles have been looked at and for how long. The same option could also be implemented if the paper is mailed to the user by automatically generating a mail back to the publisher the next time the user is online. This mail would contain all the information about which articles have been viewed for how long.

As always, passive customization does not allow the same bullet-proof insights as you get when you ask the customer directly. In this case the time that a reader has looked at an article is taken as a measure of how closely he has read it, which can be useful for funnelling related articles to him. In most cases this might be a fairly good approximation. But what if the reader has only just started to read the article when his telephone suddenly rings and he becomes involved in a conversation? When he comes back to the computer ten minutes later and decides that he is not interested in the article, the computer has already recorded ten minutes' viewing time. As always, in the absence of active customization, passive customization is much better than nothing. Nevertheless, any web site should always strive to make active customization as easy and hassle free as possible, because active customization provides more reliable insights into what the user really wants.

The Personal Journal is proof that news can be sold on the Internet instead of providing it free

A good example of a customized newspaper is the Personal Journal of the Wall Street Journal, available by monthly subscription (*www.wsj.com*). The web site allows the user to select articles on specific areas of interest or on specific companies. He can add the stocks that are of interest to him and can even select an email alert for breaking news. The Personal Journal is easy to configure and works instantly after the first registration. It is also proof that news can be sold on the Internet instead of providing it free.

The success of Personal Journal raises significant questions about the nature of periodicals of all kinds. Readers will have considerable choice about the amount of information they want to receive, the level of detail and the frequency of delivery – all of these factors can just as easily be tailored to the individual reader as the content of the paper. A customized journal could deliver the stock prices for selected companies on a daily or even hourly basis, whereas new political developments might be reported only biweekly so the subscriber can keep up some semblance of interest in the wider world to avoid embarrassment at business dinners. Across the top the user might want the current weather forecast to be displayed before weekends and public holidays so he can plan his free time.

A publication's competency lies in digging up, verifying, and writing about information of interest to its readers. This staff competence is generally confined to certain fields – say, fashion for *Vogue* and business for the *Financial Times* – although most daily newspapers have more general credentials. This specialization limits its credibility when it attempts to extend its brand to additional readers. If you are selling the *Financial Times*, no matter how customized you get, you are probably not going to gain many *In Style* readers by doing a special FT report on Cindy Crawford's furniture. The brand name probably does not have that kind of magic.

Customization, therefore, is only possible within the target group. However, by customizing within the target group, a business publication has an opportunity to expand its initial audience by targeting everyone who is interested in business and might be attracted to the name. It also might help gain additional relationships with those who already read the publication – say a special issue on a particular business, or a chance to chat online with a well-known expert in a particular field.

Branding is even more important on the impersonal Internet than it is in the bricks and mortar world. Because of the astronomical growth of the web, and the glut of information on it, people will retreat to trusted brands out of sheer information overload and confusion. Implementing transaction capabilities is the cheapest thing about the Internet. The most expensive is building a brand image and designing and implementing systems for customization that will make the brand distinctive.

Establishing a strong brand goes way beyond advertising. The total customer experience counts: the design of the homepage, customization, number of clicks to reach the desired page, fulfilment accuracy, prompt emails to confirm delivery status – the list goes on and on. This can be a challenge for multi-channel retailers because many options that can be offered through the web cannot be offered through traditional sales channels where customization would be prohibitively expensive or impossible to implement. This mismatch makes it difficult to communicate the different sales channels for the product as part of a single brand.

Branding is even more important on the impersonal Internet than it is in the bricks and mortar world

The objective of a customized interface is to increase sales volume and push high-margin products. However, the emphasis on high-margin products should not equate with pushing expensive products in the customer's mind. For example, travel agents do not make a lot of money on transatlantic flights; the margins on hotel bookings and car rentals are considerably higher. When a customer who books a flight from London to Miami is also offered a hotel and a rental car for a reasonable price, he will probably consider this a convenient one-stop service instead of suspecting that the travel agent only wants to push high-margin products.

Similarly, when the customer buys coffee beans at a web site, a typical loss leader, the system could then ask if he needs higher-margin coffee filters. Again, the customer who is thus reminded will probably see this as a helpful hint, not as a crafty way to cross-sell a high-margin product. In this way, cross-selling, if it is used properly, can not only increase share of wallet, but can also boost profitability. Conversely, if the customer comes to a web site to buy coffee filters, the retailer would be wise not to ruin his margin by reminding the customer that he might also need coffee. The example shows that a customized and interactive user interface can be very effective in increasing the share of wallet and the profitability of this customer.

Customized mailings

Once you have obtained information about users who surfed your web site you can also start to use customized mailings. The same customized information that attracted the customer to your screen can also be used for mailings to get him to return. This is not the same as a cold mailing, because for cold mailings you do not know enough about the customer to be able to send a meaningful message. Cold mailings are a scatter gun approach; customized mailings are rifles.

Mailings to the customer and the interactive web site design, therefore, must be closely interlinked because most of the information for effective mailings will come from surfing and buying patterns. Once the retailer has obtained information about a customer, he can begin communicating meaningfully with that person. The difference between customized mailings and 'spam', the Internet slang for impersonal mass mailings, lies in the relevance for the customer. If 19 out of 20 email messages the customer receives from the retailer are totally irrelevant, he will remove himself from that retailer's mailing list as quickly as possible. If 15 out of 20 messages are of interest because they actually address the customer's needs, he will probably look forward to the next message. Therefore, meaningful communication should be rooted in information about the individual customer's interests and preferences. Be sure that he considers your emails useful: otherwise your web site loses credibility and, in the end, you lose the customer.

The objective of customized mailings is to bring the customer back to the web site. The easiest and least expensive way to communicate with the customer offline is to send him an email; that is why it is so vital to obtain the customer's correct email address as quickly as possible. If the customer does not come back to the web site on his own and the retailer does not have his email address, it becomes much more expensive – and in many cases virtually unfeasible – to contact him again.

From the knowledge that the retailer has collected about the customer, he should be able to craft a message that will induce the customer to revisit the web site. The more accurate and detailed the information, the greater the opportunity to create an interesting offer. A self-reinforcing cycle evolves: the better you know the customer, the more focused your customized mailings, the higher the chance that the customer will visit the web site again, the more information you can collect about the customer and the better your ability to send even more focused messages – and so on.

In order to ensure that this cycle is actually self-reinforcing, the company also has to be able to measure which email led to what kind of customer response. Current offline communication media are not adapted to capturing digitized information. When a bank, for example, sends you a direct mail letter about a new service, it is very difficult for the company to find out how you reacted to the letter. Imagine that such a letter was focused exactly on your needs and you decided to buy the product. The direct mail centre might never learn if you decided to go to one of their branches to close the deal instead of calling a freephone number or responding by mail. Customized mailings on the Internet, however, make it possible to track the precise response allowing the cycle to be closed.

The ability to measure responses to customized mailings digitally helps to focus mailings more and more precisely. It also offers the opportunity to experiment with different types of mailings and mailing schedules. Varying email times might be an interesting feature to experiment with for customers who are online all the time at work. For example, if you send emails in batches during the night, they might have to compete for the recipient's attention with dozens of others first thing in the morning, all of which are work related and therefore take priority. But if you send an email right after lunch, when most people are going through a lull, they might be very appreciative for any excuse to put down work. This also has the advantage that your message arrives by itself instead of buried in a flurry of other messages.

For people who are not continuously online, the day of the week might also be important, because it will affect how promptly they respond. Would your customers rather read their messages on the weekend or in the middle of the night? Once the customer reads your message and fails to react immediately, you have already lost half the battle. She might put the message aside in some folder with the intention to read it more closely later, but chances are she will never get around to it. Of course sending the message at a certain time of the day is easy for email addresses of people who live in the same time zone. To get it right in the USA or Australia might be a bit more challenging.

Customized emails are essentially one-to-one communication and should contain information so valuable or interesting that they lead inevitably to the customer's return to the web site

The effectiveness of customized mailings is enhanced if they are focused on existing customers who have requested (or at least agreed to receive) your marketing messages. The key differentiation criterion is the information you have about your customer. Who knows what about whom determines how you can customize your mailings. Just capturing the email address is not enough. Email is not a very good medium by which to communicate brand marketing or send generic messages that no one really likes. Customized emails are essentially one-to-one communication and should contain information so valuable or interesting that they lead inevitably to the customer's return to the web site.

If the customer would actually prefer not to get any more emails from you, there should always be an easy option to stop them. Many sites where you can request emails about certain subjects will explain at the outset how to take your name off the mailing list of the service. That is a good start. But by the time the user actually wants to cancel, few will remember those instructions or will be able to find the initial mail that explained how. As a consequence, the next time they think about subscribing to an email service or even giving away their email address they will be much less forthcoming.

The inability easily to stop unwanted email can be overcome by communicating right from the start that every mail will contain a one-click option to prevent further mailings. Every mail could also contain a message like: 'If you want to receive messages about a different subject please click here' or 'If you do not want to receive messages from us any more please click here.'

The first reaction of many companies to this proposal will be dismay because they understandably fear that their email list, which has cost them so much effort to accumulate, will shrink by 90 per cent within the first week. But think again. If the customers are not interested in the information that you are mailing them there is no point in forcing those mails on to their desktops. They will be thrown out without having been opened, and simultaneously they will annoy the customer every single time he has to drag one to the recycle bin. Sending email to a large but unfocused email list is still shooting with pellets. In the age of the Internet this is no longer necessary.

If you think you are sending customized mailings based on the tastes and needs of the individual customers only to find out that half the recipients cancel immediately, you did something wrong in the first place. Either you do not know enough about the customer to create an interesting message or you have drawn the wrong conclusions from your information. In either case, your mailing was customized incorrectly. But even this experience can be useful because it teaches you more about what you are doing. Therefore, you should not be afraid of offering a cancellation option. It is part of the customization of the site.

The issue of active and passive customization once again enters the equation. In this case, active customization refers to a user actively requesting information about specific products or services as they become available. Let us say the user enters a real estate web site and searches for two-bedroom apartments in downtown Frankfurt with a little garden and which permit pets. Currently, the real estate agent might have nothing available in this category. But he can ask the user if he wants to be notified as soon as an apartment that meets the criteria becomes available. At the same time the real estate agent could send an email to all owners of two-bedroom apartments that meet these specifications that there is a prospective tenant. Depending on how long the apartment has already been vacant some landlords might consider waiving their initial condition of 'no pets allowed'.

Every time the user performs a search on a particular web site the site could offer the option of notifying the user if other products that meet the user's criteria become available. If the customer asks to be notified when a special product becomes available, the web site has all the necessary information to contact him because the customer has specified the criteria he is looking for. There is no danger of sending an irrelevant message. On the contrary, a notification on request would probably be perceived as enhanced service and a convenience by most customers.

If there is no way to get a customer to request information about special products by email, there is still the option of using passive customization for productive communication. As always with passive customization there is a danger of sending messages that are irrelevant for the customer and therefore an annoyance. In this case it is very important to have collected enough information about the customer to create a meaningful message. The more customers take advantage of active customization the more information the web site has for passive customization.

Imagine that British Airways finds out from analyzing active customization requests that most people who fly on business every week and collect thousands of frequent traveller miles prefer to use their miles on short weekend breaks to fancy destinations in southern Europe with their spouses. If 20 per cent of all frequent travellers between the age of 30 and 35 living in London have asked to be notified when there is a weekend vacancy for two people from London to Nice, Paris or Rome, the airline might want to test whether other travellers with high mile account balances might be interested in the same kind of information. Therefore, active customization is invaluable input information for passive customization. As we will see later, active product customization can also be very valuable for providing information for product design for mass production.

All types of mailings have the ultimate aim of getting the customer back on to the web site to buy a product or service, sooner or later

Customized mailings, active or passive, fall in several different categories. They can inform about special product availability or remind about special timing, they can answer personal questions or they can give information about ordered products. The following sections describe the different types of mailings briefly. All types of mailings have the ultimate aim of getting the customer back on to the web site to buy a product or service, sooner or later. Depending on the kind of business, there are various ways of inducing customers to return to web sites. Remember, however, that customers must always think that emails from retailers are valuable.

Product availability

One way to induce the customer to come back to the web site is to inform him about availability of products or services the retailer knows are of special interest to the customer. As outlined earlier this can be because the customer has requested this kind of information or because the retailer has deduced from the customer's behaviour that he would be interested in this product. This kind of email only makes sense if the product or service is not readily available at all times. An example would be certain flights that are available only occasionally, books that are out of print or products that are offered at a special price.

One way to make sure the customer makes his way to the web site promptly is to offer a low-price product, perhaps a loss leader, for a limited period of time. This also ensures that the retailer does not have to sell too many loss leaders to customers who happen to be on the web site for other reasons. Of course, this will be profitable only if the customer also buys other products at the web site. If the analysis of buying patterns shows that certain customers only come to the site to buy specials and nothing else, consider excluding them from future campaigns because while they are increasing revenue, they are actually decreasing profits.

Efforts at cross-selling are especially effective if the company knows that important events have taken place in the customer's life that will change the way he leads it

Any customized communication always has to meet the criterion of being relevant for the customer. When offering a loss leader there is a particular danger of sending the email to everyone on your email list without analyzing whether the product is relevant for all those customers. Remember that a diaper offer way below cost is a bargain only for people with babies.

Cross-selling

Another form of customized emails is those that inform about products that are related to other products that have already been purchased, for purposes of cross-selling. Here the information is not about product availability because the product is available for the same price at any time. The value added for the customer is to receive succinct, pertinent information at a particular moment. Efforts at cross-selling are especially effective if the company knows that important events have taken place in the customer's life that will change the way he leads it, such as starting a new job, marriage, birth of a child or buying a house. Different products lend themselves to different kinds of cross-sales that must be analyzed differently.

Let us take the example of buying a house. The real estate agent from whom you bought the house has a great deal more information about you than the simple fact that you purchased it. He knows the price and something about your income and net worth so he can estimate the kind of money you will be willing to spend on other things. Someone who has just rented a one-bedroom apartment for £200 a month will not be willing to spend as much on a kitchen as someone who has just bought a four-bedroom house for £500,000. He knows you have just bought a house that does not have a modern kitchen, so chances are that you will care about contractors who can build high-quality kitchens relatively quickly. He even knows the dimensions of the existing kitchen.

If the real estate agent teams up with a kitchen centre he can offer a kitchen exactly suited to the customer's needs. In an email the kitchen centre would offer a design that makes perfect use of the available room in the price range that would be expected for someone who has just spent £500,000 on a house and that can be delivered within a reasonable amount of time. Such an offer will most likely be seen as valuable information or customer service instead of as a nuisance email.

Reminders

Another efficient method of email communication is to remind the customer of something important. For example, if the customer used a car dealer's web site to book an appointment to get her car serviced, the dealer can remind the customer via email the next time the car needs an inspection and propose possible appointment dates. The customer only has to select one and press the reply key and the dealer has gained customer loyalty.

Another favourite is a florist's or jeweller's reminder of the spouse's birthday or wedding anniversary the year after an earlier purchase. If you run a web site selling such things, reminding customers of upcoming occasions, together with gift suggestions within the price range, is a very effective way to secure customer loyalty and profitable return business.

The retailer can offer the customers the option of recurring reminders or he can just remind the customer anyway. Obviously, if the customer actively deselects the option of receiving reminders no emails should be sent. As always with passive customization there is the danger of sending a message that has been rendered inappropriate by events, say the loss of a job, or a divorce.

Customer problems

Personal answers to customer queries or complaints are the ultimate customization. This is also the most expensive variant of all customized mailings, because someone actually has to write the answer. If you are selling a fairly expensive, high-margin product it should certainly be worth it. But even a low-margin commodity might justify the expense if you treat the mails as valuable customer feedback. You find out exactly what problems your customers have and can act accordingly. This can be anything from putting FAQs (Frequently Asked Questions) on your web site, to redesigning parts of the web site, to redesigning or adding to your product offering. Once you view emails from your customers as free market research delivered to your doorstep, the cost of answering will seem small compared to the free feedback that you get. We will go into detail on the value of customer feedback in a later chapter.

> **Personal answers to customer queries or complaints are the ultimate customization**

Order status

There is also the possibility of using mailing to notify of delivery status. In that case the primary objective is to give the customer peace of mind and not to bring him right back to the web site. Nevertheless, confirming emails are very important for the customer because they put him at ease that everything is working as expected. In the impersonal Internet where the computer screen is the only means of interaction this is very important. If a customer types in an order and presses the confirm button, he wonders what is going to happen next. Did the company receive the order or did the line break down in the middle of the data transfer? Was the information stored correctly? Is the product available? When will it be delivered? Was the price information correct? The customer might have all those questions and without emails to keep him informed, he might have to live in suspense for days or weeks.

> **This is a good example of how to transfer workload from the retailer to the customer while adding perceived convenience, reducing cost and increasing customer service**

So, as a minimum, you should at least send two confirmation emails to the customer. After the customer has placed an order you should place one within seconds that sends a confirmation of the order, recording all details of the order and stating an expected delivery date. That way the customer knows that you have his email address recorded correctly along with all other details of the order.

This is also a good example of how to transfer workload from the retailer to the customer while adding perceived convenience, reducing cost and increasing customer service. The customer checks to see if the order is recorded correctly, which is reassuring, and at the same time reduces the cost of correcting errors. It is a win-win situation.

The second important email message should be sent once the order has been shipped. The message should include the FedEx or UPS shipment number, so the customer has all the information he needs to check what happened in case the package does not arrive in time. In addition, this tying together of the retailer and the shipper networks is an example of how the Internet can strengthen the business proposition for all concerned. The FedEx shipment number has to be transferred from the logistics company to the book retailer to the customer in a readable format, in spite of the various systems that may be involved. This could only be effected through the open technology that lies at the heart of the web, and previously was not economically feasible.

Why not let the customer design all the communication that he receives from you?

Reassuring emails are especially important to the first-time customers who do not know who they are dealing with. They should receive confirmations on every execution step as a default option. However, they should be given a choice of specifying which order status confirmation options they would like to receive as the relationship develops. If the customer has already ordered from you several times and knows that you always keep your promises, he might choose not to receive routine confirming emails but only be notified when things do not go as planned.

Customized communication can also mean letting the customer design the way you communicate with him. We have already talked about active customization that uses information acquired from customer requests to offer certain products or services as soon as they become available. But why not let the customer design all the communication that he receives from you?

Take the example of the invoice. For consumers it probably makes little difference what an invoice looks like as long as the price is correct. For corporate accounts, however, the situation is different. A customer who works for the marketing department of a large corporation might order a PC for his department from your web site. The invoice is paid by the accounting department, however. For this transaction to go smoothly, the invoice might have to include certain company-specific details like charge numbers and the employee number of the person who ordered the PC. One company might want any discounts and freight costs to be itemized whereas another wants a single sum. Or they might want all the items listed separately but the price in one lump sum.

Whatever preferences the customer has, it costs you very little to offer these options because once the systems are installed, all the work is done by the customer. This will also save your call centre considerable time because if the options are not available on the web site you will have him on the phone asking for his invoice to be designed differently.

Everything we have discussed so far refers to customisation either by the customer himself or by the company that runs the web site. There is a third possibility, which is to get one customer to send a mail to another potential customer. An 'alert a friend' programme gives the customer the opportunity to mail a certain page, article or offer to a friend. In this case your customers actually do the customizing for you. Since their own name shows up

The beauty of this concept lies in the fact that people about whom you know absolutely nothing will receive a customized mailing about your web site

as the sender of the mail they will most likely only send it to someone they think might be interested. The message has a much better chance of getting the recipient's attention because it has been mailed by a friend and might also contain some personal information, as well as an explanation as to why that particular link might be interesting.

This option is especially important if your clientele is composed substantially of web fanatics – they enjoy showing off all the hot web sites. For you, the beauty of this concept lies in the fact that people about whom you know absolutely nothing will receive a customized mailing about your web site.

Customized advertising

There are generally two different types of web advertising. You can either advertise your web site itself or you can advertise your products and services, with links to the site. If you are advertising your web site to people who have never visited it before, it is very difficult to customize the ads. Knowledge about the other person is always the basis for customization and if they have never visited your site you will have very little knowledge about them, unless you get the information from another site – a topic we will discuss later.

Advertising the web site is very important for drawing first-time visitors

Nevertheless, advertising the web site is very important

for drawing first-time visitors. Currently, few Internet companies use print or TV or other offline media to promote their web sites, although it is becoming increasingly common in the USA. Most established companies will readily print their web address on their promotional material but will not go as far as actively promoting the site itself.

Very few companies outside the USA actively use offline media to attract people to their web sites, apart from online brokers and portals. Instead, most Internet companies use online media such as banner ads or links between sites. With banner ads and links, however, you will only reach people who are already on the Internet. Since the online population grows minute to minute, advertising in offline media might be an interesting way to attract novices directly to your site. Who knows? They might even be enticed by your advertising to take the online plunge after years of indecision.

Nevertheless, as has been mentioned before, the real benefits of customization can only be realized when the company already has preliminary information about the customer, and therefore even customized advertising is an imprecise tool for generating new traffic. It is, however, an interesting tool to draw customers back on to the site for cross-selling.

Not surprisingly customized advertising is actually a combination of both customized user interface and customized mailings of the kind we have already discussed. The reason, as we explain in a different chapter, lies in the fact that advertising for third parties can actually be a considerable revenue stream for a web site. Essentially a form of sponsorship, in the manner of commercial broadcasting, the whole business model can be built solely on selling advertisements.

The advantages of customized advertising are twofold: first of all the companies that are paying for ads are more willing to pay per hit if they can be sure that their advertisements are targeted to a pre-selected group of customers with some kind of demonstrable interest in that product. Second, potential customers who receive the customized advertising are less annoyed and more receptive, which leads to higher acceptance and higher buying ratios.

> **Essentially a form of sponsorship, in the manner of commercial broadcasting, the whole business model can be built solely on selling advertisements**

It would actually be possible to make a business profitable just by offering customized advertising for third parties. Since customized ads actually have a value for the customer because they save time, customers might register with a specific web site that has nothing but advertising. The web site would ask for the email address and for specific areas of interest. If someone wants to buy a new car and check out the current best offers, she could register at the advertising web site and immediately receive all advertisements concerning cars that fit her criteria.

This advertising on demand becomes actually very close to a search engine, depending on how specific the criteria are that the user sets. The web site ***www.yesmail.com*** is an example of a site that basically does nothing but manage, channel and customize advertising. Users register at Yesmail and select products about which they would like to receive advertisements. Yesmail sells this knowledge of several million registered users to the companies that want to be represented. Marketers are allowed to direct their message to the customer without ever seeing the customer's email address and therefore can only access the customer through Yesmail. The web site gets paid every time a member actually receives one of those advertisements. If the customer decides to change his personal online profile and deselects a certain product range, he will not receive emails about those products any more.

In addition Yesmail offers value-added services for both customers and marketers. Besides mailing the customer the advertising he wants, Yesmail also keeps track of all email lists and newsletters the user has subscribed to. By using Yesmail software the user can keep track of all lists he is on and easily remove his name from unwanted ones. For the marketers Yesmail offers another service. Each time Yesmail.com sends an email to a member it watches what they click and what they do not click. For this information marketers will pay a premium, because it helps them get quick feedback on where to allocate marketing dollars.

The difference between advertising and customer communication and information in this case actually becomes very slim

The difference between advertising and customer communication and information in this case actually becomes very slim. As advertising becomes more customized, it is perceived less as advertising and more as information worth paying for. Actively customized advertising, for which the customer has defined exactly what kind of information he wants to receive, becomes almost indistinguishable from customized mailings or customized content, because customized advertising might actually be perceived by the user as value-added content.

If none of your readers wants to see your customized advertising, you must be doing something wrong in the customization process

You could also make advertising optional for the user, of course. If you are selling an online paper, the user can choose between a less expensive version with advertising and a more expensive version without advertising. As the publisher of an online paper, you already need a lot of information about your customers because otherwise you could not customize it. This information can also be used to customize your advertising. If none of your readers wants to see your customized advertising, however, you must be doing something wrong in the customization process. If the ads are actually customized most readers should find it valuable and not readily give it up.

In any case you can only start to sell advertising once you have generated considerable traffic on your web site. This is even more true when you are selling customized advertising. Since customized advertising will only be seen by a limited number of customers who fulfil certain criteria, you have to build a much larger pool of customers in order to create an interesting offer for advertisers.

Many people have started to call the available space on the screen 'real estate', an apt comparison. Basically, a blank screen in the Internet is the same as an undeveloped parcel of land in the middle of nowhere. In itself it is worth very little. If someone builds a mall on that land, and finds the right anchor tenant, the same land suddenly becomes a popular destination. The shoppers it draws are an enticement to additional merchants, and they fill the remaining space with complementary retailers. A case in point is IKEA. The Swedish furniture house knows that it will create heavy traffic wherever it opens a new store, making the land around it more valuable. Therefore, when IKEA wants to open a new store it also buys the land around the future store and sells it to other companies later at considerably higher prices.

Likewise, a blank screen or a web site that generates little traffic is worth basically nothing. However, as the traffic grows, so does the value of that screen real estate because it can be used for banner ads or links to other web sites that generate revenue.

Once you have generated traffic and collected valuable information about your customers, the next important thing is to make the best use of your new assets. The value of banner ads and links increases as you learn more about the particular customer because the greater knowledge allows you to customize the advertising.

Imagine the web site of a real estate agent that generates a lot of traffic and sells banner ads for books. Such ads rely purely on the fact that of the thousands of people who will see the advertisement, a few will buy a book, but without any feel for how many might be readers. This is virtually the same way advertising was done before the time of the Internet. In fact, it is still done that way on highways, where billboards are placed without regard for who is actually seeing them. Say you place a billboard for Smirnoff vodka on a busy road. There is always the possibility that the people who see it either avoid drinking before they drive or do not drink at all.

The real estate web site actually has a lot more specific information about the customer. It has details on what kind of apartment or house the customer is looking for, what size, what area, what price range, with garden or without, with kitchen or without, and so on. So it could sell advertisements that are a lot more specific. For cramped city apartments, there could be ads for books on decorating on a budget, or space-saving ideas. For suburban homes on capacious lots, there could be books on landscaping.

Another example is **www.theknot.com**. The Knot is a community for couples who want to get married. It offers information and advice on all aspects of wedding plans, from choosing the perfect location to the text for invitations. A big part is devoted to helping the bride choose the right wedding gown. It offers a huge database of over 10,000 gowns that can be searched by various criteria from a 'Queen Anne neckline' to a 'mermaid silhouette'. When you find the design you want, the site directs you to the manufacturer, although you cannot order online. It will link you to all manufacturers so that you may order their individual catalogues. By giving gownmakers the opportunity to mail their catalogues directly to the bride, the Knot has broken down barriers between prospective brides and manufacturers. Before the existence of the Internet it was very difficult for the manufacturers of bridal gowns actually to get hold of addresses of brides-to-be because they had to deal with them through representatives. The catalogue mailing service of the Knot, which is nothing more than advertising on request, is therefore highly valuable to the bride and the manufacturer, and costs the Knot very little.

Another good example is the sales of any product that can only be used together with another product. Take DVD players. A DVD player by itself is not much fun – you need the discs to play on it. But since the technology is fairly new and it is likely this would be your first DVD player, chances are you do not have a large, prized collection of discs, so the next logical thing to do is buy the DVDs. So an advertisement for DVDs and a link to an appropriate web site are a logical anticipation of customer needs.

American Express offers still a further example of customized advertising. As a credit and charge card company, Amex has access to an incredible, and

> **As the traffic grows, so does the value of that screen real estate because it can be used for banner ads or links to other web sites that generate revenue**

sometimes threatening, amount of information about every one of its customers. That information is used extensively for customized advertising to accompany the credit card bills. When you have stayed in a certain hotel and paid with your American Express card you will find information about special offers or loyalty programmes from that hotel chain on your next bill. If you live in a city and spend a lot of money on expensive dining you will find information about specials in exclusive restaurants in that city on your bill. American Express can even check how successful the advertisements are if you actually go to the restaurant and pay with your American Express card. So by continuously analyzing your buying patterns the credit card company can customize its advertising of partner companies more and more to your needs.

This information-gathering capability can also be a cause of concern. You can see the potential for abuse, if these buying patterns are sold to others without the customer's knowledge. Confidential treatment of the information you gather about the customer is one of the most important preconditions for successful customized advertising.

Chapter 11

Value-added information

The customer is probably going to buy at whichever web site he happens to be on at the moment he actually makes the purchase decision. Value-added information can help ensure it is your web site

Value-added information is information that the user would usually require before making a purchase decision, but that is not related directly to the product or service for sale. Of course any web site has to describe the product or service that it sells fully. But that might not be enough to stay ahead of the competition. If you and your competitor are selling a very similar product for almost the same price, the customer is probably going to buy at whichever web site he happens to be on at the moment he actually makes the purchase decision. Value-added information can help ensure it is your web site.

The idea of value-added information is to build a relationship with the potential customer *before* he makes the decision to buy. Value-added information can help the user select the product or provide information on how to use it. If the user is on your web site to obtain this kind of information, the chances increase significantly that he will also buy at your site, if he decides to buy at all.

If the business model of the web site is built solely on attracting traffic in order to sell advertisements, the designation 'value-added information' is probably not quite correct. In that case, the content of the site as a whole should be attractive enough for the potential customer to revisit. Nevertheless, for advertising-funded web sites the same principles apply as for value-added information.

> **The customer does not really care that there are 500 other variants of the same product**

Value-added information helps to increase traffic on your site because once your helpful reputation is established, people will return when they have problems or need further information. The primary goal, however, is not to increase traffic but to increase the conversion of browsers to customers. When a customer enters a web site he is often not quite sure if he wants to buy the product at all or what specifications he would actually need to address his problem. He may not even be clear what he wants or needs.

As we will see when we discuss customized production, merely offering many different product options is not the same as adding valuable information for the customer. The customer might be confused or put off when overwhelmed by the choices. He wants the product that suits his needs. The web site operator would ideally be able to read his mind and show only that particular product. Short of that, the web site must function as an online sales assistant, listening to vague ideas and steering the customer to 'just the right thing'. The customer does not really care that there are 500 other variants of the same product. Choice in itself is not an indication of high customer orientation or high value added. What makes the choices valuable is help in selecting the right one and this is where value-added information and in some cases even expert systems come into the picture.

Solving the customer's problem goes beyond just selling a product. The company has to understand what the customer's real problem is and how he thinks before being able to design a web site that will cater to the customer's needs. In the following sections we look at value-added information based on product selection and product usage processes.

Necessary information

The most important and difficult step when designing value-added information for product selection is to determine which information your potential customers need before they decide to buy. The second step is actually to supply that information on the web site. Since it might be information that is only tangentially related to your product, this can also pose quite a challenge, especially when you have to ensure that the information is up to date. But what is value-added information for your company may be the core business of another company, creating the possibility of joining forces and integrating your web sites into a seamless flow of information and fulfilment. As long as that seamless flow is there the customer does not care or even have to notice that the information is available on one site and the actual purchase is on another.

What is value-added information for your company may be the core business of another company

The buyer's need can be identified and triggered by value-added information on one web site and directed to a product purchase site. Someone might come to the information site with a rather unclear idea of what he wants or needs. Through systematic exploration of value-added information technology, the needs can be identified. By the time the customer actually makes the decision to buy, he has arrived at the retailer's web site.

For example, if the customer's objective is to prepare a special dinner for guests, he'll usually decide on a recipe first and then buy the necessary ingredients. When an online supermarket offers recipes and the customer finds one he likes, the chances increase that he will also buy the ingredients from that web site. The retailer caters to the customer's desire for convenience by anticipating and satisfying that customer's information needs. Assuming that the customer is a good enough cook actually to execute the recipe well enough to please his guests, he will return to the web site the next time he wants to entertain, and for more routine shopping as well.

By offering mouth-watering recipes and providing the convenience of putting the right amount of every ingredient into the shopping basket with one mouse click, the retailer has a strong tool with which to increase his share of that customer's wallet. A 'recipe of the month' containing higher-margin products displayed prominently on the homepage also allows the retailer to promote those particular ingredients.

To acquire the necessary breadth and quality of recipes the retailer might have to form a strategic alliance with another company. However, in order to obtain the full benefit from the alliance, the value-added information must be fully incorporated into the retailer's web site and interact with the retailer's offerings. For example, simple links from a web site with recipes to a web site for groceries, where the customer has to key in all the recipe's ingredients again, are likely neither to impress the user nor to enforce customer satisfaction or retention; what seems like such a surefire alliance may very likely turn customers off if the implemented technology fails to deliver.

The retailer caters to the customer's desire for convenience by anticipating and satisfying that customer's information needs

When thinking about what information the customer might need before deciding on a product, some companies have to think beyond the obvious. Recipes for food retailers are a natural. Neighbourhood school information for real estate agents might seem a little more far fetched at first sight, but in New York, being zoned for a particular neighbourhood school can mean a difference of hundreds of thousands of dollars in house prices, even with homes of equal quality situated only a block apart.

One day in the future, the web sites of real estate agents could offer direct links to the web sites of schools, so the customer can have an online look at the future school and its offering for their children if they decide to move to that area. This could be supplemented by third-party ratings of schools. And if the schools themselves have web sites, there could be links to real estate agents in the neighbourhood, for those families that search for schools first before they decide to move.

The information could be refined further, to encompass secondary child-oriented information, such as athletic teams, music lessons and playgrounds. Many neighbourhood enthusiasts, parenting networks and local institutions such as churches and synagogues have created their own web sites, all of which could have links. Even if a different real estate agent offers the customer a house that he likes in a different area, the chances are that the customer will return to the initial web site for the value-added information, giving the first agent a chance to offer listings of his own in the new area. And, of course, coming back to the idea of customized communication, the school information might not be so prominently displayed if the customer is searching for studios or one-bedroom apartments and is thus less likely to have children.

Consulting or assistance to help consumers find the best products can be an important customization feature. For a web site operator, this can even entail designing an expert system that leads the user through the different steps of designing the product. The value-added information in this instance would be very close to the online sales assistant we described earlier.

Value-added information can also mean offering functions that make it easier for the customer to make a decision. Let us return to the example of the customer who wants to install a new kitchen. The constraints are the shape of the room and the budget. Anything else is basically open to discussion. In the bricks and mortar world the customer now has to go to a kitchen store, select a kitchen type, have the sales assistant design the kitchen with the available parts in that kitchen type and calculate a price. The whole thing is time consuming, involving laborious discussions and hours spent poring over catalogues and looking at samples at the store during your normal work hours. In the online world, however, the web site of a kitchen retailer could offer easy-to-handle online design tools that would also, of course, be available during all hours of the night.

The software lets you move cupboards, stoves and refrigerators on the screen and then shows you the complete kitchen from a 3-D perspective, in colour, with the current price and actual delivery time – every time you make a change. That way you can easily design your own kitchen online and also make sure you know the implication of every little change for the total price and the delivery time. This

Consulting or assistance to help consumers find the best products can be an important customization feature

would make the design and decision-making process a lot easier, faster and self-controlled. The chances that you will take the printout of your kitchen design to a competitor to be built are rather slim, especially if the price is right. Besides, once you have designed your kitchen on the web site, have entered all relevant information and are prompted with price and delivery time, you are just one click away from buying the kitchen. Shopping for a cheaper contract would not be worth the time it would take, especially since the online kitchen store could offer very competitive prices. After all, the customer has taken over most of the time-consuming work of designing the kitchen himself.

This is exactly what value-added information is designed to do: attract the customer to the web site and lead him through a series of steps in his decision-making process until he is actually ready to make a buying decision. The chances are high that he will buy on that site.

The virtual sales assistant – and the real designers behind the software – could also help you and make suggestions concerning the design of the kitchen. She might alert you to the fact that the dishwasher is quite far away from the sink which will lead to inefficient work processes in the future kitchen. She might also suggest

When helping the customer make a decision about selecting the product the retailer obviously has the opportunity to influence the decision towards his own product portfolio

things that you might want to add, thus giving the retailer cross-selling opportunities.

When helping the customer make a decision about selecting the product the retailer obviously has the opportunity to influence the decision towards his own product portfolio. By the same token, the choices that the retailer offers have to be wide enough to be taken seriously by the customer. If the retailer only offers one type of kitchen, the customer might like the design function of the web site but will look at other sites for alternatives, both on design and on prices. If the retailer's web site already offers kitchens from 30 different manufacturers the customer has a better feel for the wider marketplace and might be less likely to shop around.

Regardless, the web offers the possibility of developing new ways to determine what the customer actually wants. In some cases, the customer might find it very difficult to put his tastes and needs into words. If someone is furnishing a house for the first time, she might not have a very clear idea of what she wants. Imagine an interior design web site that can be used free of charge but that is linked to major furniture shops. The web site generates revenue on a commission basis every time a customer buys furniture at one of the associated shops, much in the way decorators and designers operate in the traditional marketplace, by selling at retail the furnishings they are privileged to buy at discount. The web site would provide suggestions for different possibilities for furnishing the different rooms.

The user first keys in the number and size of rooms, the location of doors and windows and the overall budget. With a user-friendly interface that part should not be much of a problem for the user. The next thing the web site has to do is determine what styles the user likes. For people who have not studied interior design, answering these questions might be difficult, impossible even. Most have probably not given much thought to the styles they prefer, at least to be able to name them. But everyone can usually tell you straight away whether he likes a certain design or not when he sees it. So instead of asking a question such as 'Would you prefer a carpet in a light or dark colour?' which is really difficult to answer when you have no idea what colour the wall is, and what it looks like together with a red sofa, the web site could use examples. In this case the user would be asked to view 20 or 30 pictures of fully furnished rooms and click on a scale from 'very pretty' to 'ugly' whether he likes the particular design. The pictures could include all combinations of different design styles. Once the web site has developed an idea of the general look the customer likes, it could narrow down the choices and move step by step towards the final design.

The more detailed the last steps are, the more the user can become involved in choosing individual pieces of furniture and designing the precise look. He could, for example, accept the general design for the living room, and the way the furniture is arranged, but change the colour of the curtains from dark red to light red and choose a different type of chair. Of course, the web site would only offer those choices that can be fulfilled and delivered by associated web sites. Therefore, the design site has to be associated with as many furniture houses as possible.

Once the overall design is completed the user would go on to the web sites of the different furniture retailers, preferably without knowing that he had even left the interior design web site, because of integrated information flow, and select details of the chosen products. Where the design web site might only offer a price range for the whole room, because various items might be superficially similar but in fact vary in price and other specifics, the user could now select the items piece by piece on the basis of their different features. Since the information is also linked back to the design web site, that web site would store the complete record of prices, delivery times and ordered products giving the customer a reference point for monitoring the fulfilment process.

The other reason that value-added information becomes even more important on the Internet is the number of choices that are already possible without customization

Value added information in the selection process is especially useful for the customer if the web site offers customization possibilities. The retailer has the task to help the customer through the maze of options, because otherwise you scare him away instead of impressing him with added convenience. The other reason that value-added information becomes even more important on the Internet than it is in the bricks and mortar world is the number of choices that are already possible without customization. One of the prime considerations for retailers in the bricks and mortar world is shelf space. A bookshop or CD retailer can carry only as many books or CDs as his shelves can hold. Therefore the retailer always has to do a certain pre-selection. He cannot possibly offer everything available on the market because it would go beyond the physical scope of his store.

On the Internet the four-wall limitation does not exist

On the Internet the four-wall limitation does not exist. A web site can offer 20 million items just as easily as 20,000. As in the bricks and mortar world, one of the value-added activities of a retailer is to make a pre-selection of the goods for the customer. It is just that in the case of the Internet that pre-selection can and should be different for every single customer.

Books and CDs are also a good example of another type of value-added information that can help the customer in the selection process. In order to sell books or CDs successfully, you can ask the customer what kind of reading or music she likes. Or you can offer a search engine that selects by title, subject or author. But in many cases, after a reader has finished reading a book she liked, she just wants another good book, not necessarily by the same author or about the same subject. This pre-selection is difficult to make by analytic standards. An interesting alternative is to use the accumulated preferences of other customers as a guideline.

On Amazon, when you look at a particular book, you are always shown suggestions of some other books that have been ordered by people who also bought the initial book. This is an innovative way of helping people select a book without overwhelming them with choices. The accumulated preferences of other users are especially valuable when the product quality is a matter of taste and not objective quality standards.

The important thing with value-added information is always to make sure the customer is on your site when making the decision and that there is no reason to leave the site before buying. If you are selling high-price items, cars for instance, via the web, the customer might decide to buy a particular model while she is on your site but may not be able to do so before she has talked to the bank or leasing company. Instead of letting her walk away and hoping that she will eventually return with the money (and does not decide in the meantime to buy the car somewhere else), you could consider offering financing and leasing options right there on the web site.

Educating the consumer

Some people avoid buying a product either because they are afraid that they will not be able to use it or because they see no value in using it. Early VCRs are an example – many older people were afraid they would be unable to programme them, and given the poor quality of the instructions in those days, they were right! Today, however, with so much product innovation, the chances of selling increase considerably when the customers get clear, simple information about how the product can be used.

It is short sighted to think that this information is important only after the sale, and therefore to disregard it for the sales process. Given the importance of customer loyalty on the Internet, it becomes crucial that customers actually manage to use the product properly. If they fail, they are likely not to come back or make further purchases from your site.

But even more important: customers will not make even the initial purchase if they do not know how to use the product. Only if you can offer competent instruction and advice on the use of the product will the customer feel confident enough to buy it in the first place.

Often people will not buy a product at a do-it-yourself store unless they know how to use it. Most people who have never installed ceramic tiles themselves, for example, will be reluctant to buy them over the Internet unless they know that they will eventually manage to get them installed. If you team up with a web site such as Ask the Builder (***www.askbuilder.com***) your customers can get accurate instructions on how to do the job themselves. Your customer can find out that ceramic floor tiles must be installed perfectly level, but also that, unfortunately, most floors are not level! So the web site provides step-by-step instructions on how to get it right. Once your customer has read through several well-explained tips and tricks he will feel more comfortable buying the tiles at your site and installing them himself.

virtual visit

Value-added information can also be displayed in a customized way. Do-it-yourself information can be displayed on different levels for beginners and experts. On the expert level the instructions would read 'Attach the lamp to the wall with the screws provided.' The beginner's instructions would explain everything from how to determine if there is a water or electricity line at the point where you want to drill into the wall up to what drill and what kind of plug you should use for which type of wall.

Beyond customers' fear of not being able to use a product is the fear that they will not use the product once they buy it. Imagine you are selling home trainers such as exercycles and treadmills online. One of the biggest fears that stops people buying a home trainer in the first place is that they are afraid they will not have the willpower actually to use it regularly once they have bought it. This fear is not unrealistic, since the majority of home trainers usually end up in the basement so they do not remind the owner that he failed miserably in his resolution to get in shape.

But how about a personal fitness programme that is prepared by an online fitness assistant? It could use the online community in a similar way to Weight Watchers, encouraging the individual to stick with his best intentions. The online fitness assistant could do a basic personal check-up in which the customer has to do easy exercises and feed back results such as pulse rate. Combining these with information about age and medical history, the online fitness assistant would then determine the fitness level of the individual customer.

The customer would then enter the level of fitness that he would like to achieve and the amount of time that he would like to spend each week to achieve this goal. The fitness assistant would propose a personal training plan with certain milestones, such as riding the equivalent of five kilometres on the bike within 20 minutes, with a pulse rate no higher than 120.

Once the customer has bought the home trainer, the online fitness assistant would start its programme. After setting up the personal fitness plan it would regularly send emails to the user in order to remind him of the programme for the day and ask about the work-out he has recently done. More advanced features could link the home trainer itself directly back with the web site, so the online fitness assistant would always have current information about the length of time that the home trainer is used, the work-out level and the pulse rate. The online fitness assistant can get to know the details of the customer's work-outs and more about his personal fitness. He could also regularly offer related information, such as dietary suggestions or information about the positive effects of fitness on the immune system. Such reinforcement might help the customer maintain his commitment to fitness, but without any of the personal mortification people feel when they are nagged by those they know to work out.

If the user starts to become less diligent after the first few months of enthusiasm he could be reminded regularly by email of the high level of fitness he has already achieved and how it is continuously dropping without further effort. The user could even customize the communication by determining how many reminders he would like to receive and on what level: educational, friendly, pushy or even aggressive.

The exercise equipment retailer might want to charge a monthly fee for the online trainer. Even if it could easily be offered free of charge it might be more successful if you charge a monthly fee because people tend to take things more seriously if they are paying for them. Or you could charge a monthly fee for the use of the site but offer the fitness assistant free of charge for buyers of new home trainers. The web site would remain free as long as users met their training targets – a development that would require online feedback from the usage of the bicycle to the web site. Since the aim of the whole web site is to bring the fitness success rate of the customers to a higher level, charging a fee might actually increase the success of the web site.

People tend to take things more seriously if they are paying for them

Once the value-added information mechanism is properly set up and running, the retailer would monitor the success rate of the customers in training and use that information for marketing purposes. This could be data showing that of 100 people who normally buy a home trainer, 90 per cent use it less than once a month after six months, whereas with the online programme after six months 65 per cent still use it more than twice a week. This information can then help considerably in selling the home trainer because it addresses one of the main fears of the user, as well as generating additional revenue through the online fitness assistant.

Value-added information can also be used to generate demand for a specific product. Suppose you have a web site that sells both analogue and digital cameras. Value-added information in this case could be tips and tricks on how to achieve the best results when taking pictures, particularly in special circumstances – marriage pictures inside a church, for example, or an eclipse – that could themselves be the focal point of other special promotions.

Since most people who surf on such a site would probably have a camera, the potential for new sales is not obvious. But when you start introducing new techniques that can only be achieved with new models or are even exclusively limited to digital cameras, after a while many users might feel the desire for equipment like that shown and explained on your site. Without that information they might actually have been quite happy with their old camera for another five years, but now that you have alerted them to the technical possibilities they might well decide to take the plunge. And the first place for them to look is on your site of course! Actually, from their surfing patterns you might be able to deduce that they want one of the new cameras and offer them one before the competition even finds out about it.

These are all just examples of what value-added information could mean for different businesses. Depending on what you sell you have to find the kind of information that is most valuable for your customers and as the examples in this chapter show it might be unrelated to the features of the product you are selling.

The information that the customer obtains from the web site is also useful for retailers who want to customize their offers. If a customer cannot decide between different alternatives and keeps requesting more and more information, perhaps the product variants are not designed to solve the customer's problems. If customers request reams of information about how to use a product before they buy it, perhaps the perception of the product is that it is difficult to use and possibly it should be positioned differently or redesigned.

Chapter 12

User-generated content

User-generated content can take two forms: customer feedback displayed on the web site or communication directly between users. Both can serve to build a community and can extend the value of the information the site offers. One of the most important functions of user-generated content, however, is to communicate to the users that many other people frequent this site. Think about it: have you ever been in a restaurant all by yourself with no other guests? How did you

> **User-generated content can take two forms: customer feedback displayed on the web site or communication directly between users**

feel? You probably wondered what was wrong with the restaurant – was the food that bad or was there something going on that you knew nothing about? It is not surprising that a customer on a web site might feel the same way. She might wonder if this is a trustworthy company she is buying from. Being required to key in a credit card number makes most people hesitate; can the site be trusted? They might wonder about the quality of the products and if they are actually as good as promised. And they might wonder if the company will still be around if spare parts are needed two years later.

Being required to key in a credit card number makes most people hesitate

Web-based businesses are at a disadvantage compared to bricks and mortar companies, where the customer can judge the size and seriousness of the business by the premises. If he buys at a huge department store with branches in every mall in the country, chances are that the business will still be there if the customer has a warranty complaint three months later. In these circumstances, the display of comments from other customers on a web site is greatly reassuring. There is safety in numbers.

On the Internet, however, it is difficult to judge the size of a company by its web site appearance. With the technology available today even small firms can manage to appear very professional on the net, especially when their appearance is compared to the plain, non-interactive sites of large multinational groups, many of which lack transaction capabilities and links to supplier and customer databases. It is therefore relatively easy for 'fly by night' firms which build professional-looking web sites and then take the money and run. It is much harder to fake user-generated content accumulated over several years, and this becomes an indicator of stability and seriousness of the business.

There is safety in numbers

The web gives the retailer a unique opportunity to make individual comments accessible to all customers. In many cases the information that is acquired through user-generated content could not be gathered in any other way, like reader feedback about millions of books at Amazon.com, because it would be impossible to supply such vast amounts of information unless you have thousands of people doing it for you for free.

User-generated content is especially useful for increasing both traffic and customer loyalty to a particular web site. Due to the 'law of increasing returns', a linear increase in the number of customers leads to an exponential increase in the value of the web site and, therefore, losing a customer hurts twice as much. Each additional member who takes part in the community increases the value of the site, and in turn attracts more members.

While the number of users may not mean anything to an individual when she buys something, it means a great deal if information contributed by customers is part of the value proposition. The value of the whole web site increases for all users as more of them contribute to the site and users communicate with each other. A web site that accumulates a great deal of meaningful user-generated content and hosts dozens of focused and interesting chat groups becomes increasingly attractive for new customers.

On the Internet, it is difficult to judge the size of a company by its web site appearance

At the same time, it becomes more difficult for competitors to draw customers away from such sites or even to retain their existing customers. The process rolls faster and faster once a certain critical mass is reached. This competitive advantage of user-generated content cannot easily be copied by competitors and increases the switching costs. The user can change to a different web site but he cannot take the content and his community with him to a different site. This principle highlights once again the importance of the first-mover advantage in electronic commerce.

Since user-generated content can become an essential part of the web site's value proposition, the difference between customer and supplier becomes blurred. Individuals can act as suppliers of content one day and as customers the next. Individuals create content for the site both actively and passively, through their comments on the one hand and their buying patterns on the other, which themselves become part of the value proposition of that web site.

virtual visit

Take the example of ***www.eBay.com***. eBay hosts online auctions that facilitate the exchange of goods that otherwise would only be marketable through specialist dealers, newspaper ads and collectors' organizations. What makes the auctions really valuable for individuals is that buyers and sellers also get information about one another. As we described in the chapter on certification, the rating system is provided by the web site but the content that brings the system to life is provided by the users in their comments on counterparty behaviour during transactions. The web site becomes more valuable the more people use the site and contribute to the rating system.

Due to the 'law of increasing returns', a linear increase in the number of customers leads to an exponential increase in the value of the web site and, therefore, losing a customer hurts twice as much

User-generated content provides competitive advantage that cannot easily be duplicated; once a person has accumulated a high rating as a trustworthy buyer and seller at eBay, she has little incentive to change to a different auction site where she has to start all over again. Therefore, user-generated content increases switching costs and makes it extremely difficult for competitors to win over eBay customers. Last but not least, most people who have taken the time to comment will come back to the site just to see if their comments are actually displayed and accessible. Who does not like to see his words in print?

> **While the number of users may not mean anything to an individual when she buys something, it means a great deal if information contributed by customers is part of the value proposition**

Customer feedback on the web site

Customer feedback displayed on the web site gives the retailer credibility and makes it easier for the customers to choose products or services that will actually satisfy their needs. The retailer should make it as easy as possible to contribute. The web site could offer a prepared form for the customer to fill in and email to the retailer. While many bricks and mortar retailers and businesses such as hotels and restaurants have provided questionnaires about service in postcard format in the past, the feedback is never provided to other consumers. It is for management to review and make changes.

The web gives the retailer the unique opportunity to make individual customer comments accessible for all customers at very little cost. Since the information is already digitized, the web site only has to scan it quickly in order to ensure that it is actually pertinent to the product and does not contain any offensive language and then can put it online straight away. The more customer feedback there is, the easier it becomes for new customers to make informed decisions, which increases customer satisfaction and ultimately customer retention.

Once you start integrating customer feedback into your web site, language becomes an issue. If you have offered your web site in five different languages, you are likely to get customer feedback in five different languages. Two problems arise. First of all you have to screen the feedback before you put it on your web site because you have to check the content. After all, you do not want any defamatory, unprofessional or offensive content on the site. This can be dealt with in two ways. It might require hiring people who speak those languages. However, as more web sites encounter those problems, service firms will proliferate in the different countries to screen content based on the criteria of their clients.

The second challenge is that you have to reach critical mass within each language in order to benefit from the law of increasing returns. If a travel agent's web site offers only one user comment about a particular hotel that the customer is interested in, it will be of very little help in making a decision. If a travel agent has lots of content in English but very little in Spanish and French, potential customers can still profit from the overall customer rating of the hotel that is based on English-language feedback, even if they cannot read the individual comments.

Another example is the eBay rating system. Even if you speak no English and cannot read the individual comments a particular seller received, you can still understand that a total rating of 150 points means that 150 people have been very satisfied in dealing with that person. The same is true for hotels. Even if you cannot read the individual comments of other customers, a combination of symbols and numbers can still convey ratings about categories such as sports activities and childcare facilities. Therefore, when you want to make customer feedback an important feature of your web site, you have to design it in such a way that the essence of what customers say can easily be translated into different languages.

> **You have to reach critical mass within each language in order to benefit from the law of increasing returns**

The fact that user feedback is digitized is already helpful because you can make it available for everyone at very little extra cost. But really to enhance the value, you have to structure the feedback form in such a way that you can easily analyze and interpret the results. For a travel agent this would mean that the user cannot write his whole contribution as text. He should also be asked to click on several options that gather the feedback in a more structured way. Of course, there should be a limited number of questions to click on because otherwise the user will be deterred by having to answer too many. This information can then be statistically analyzed and made available in all the different languages the web site offers. Even if you do not want to offer your web site in different languages it makes sense to capture at least some of the user-generated content in a form that can be statistically analyzed.

If your customer is searching for a hotel with scuba-diving facilities and excellent childcare while the parents go diving, the web site can provide this information. In order to determine whether the childcare facilities are 'excellent', a statistical analysis of the comments of other users will usually be more credible than other rating standards.

One alternative would be to have employees of your own company rate the facilities by inspecting them personally, which is very costly, especially if you want to keep the information up to date. Also, a brief inspection once a year will not yield the same depth of information as the cumulative reports of customers who have used the facilities for two or three weeks each all year round. Once the travel agent's web site is connected to hundreds of thousands of hotels it would take a prohibitively expensive army of evaluators continuously travelling the world to rate all facilities.

Another, and probably useless cheap method would be to take the hotel owner's word for it, which would be about as reassuring as promises from the fox standing outside the chicken coop that the chickens inside are safe! Customers, however, will give you first-hand, up-to-date information at very low cost. Customers might not be very objective in their rating, but they do not have to be in order to make the system work. Since you aggregate the opinions of a number of people on one hotel, statistically speaking the differences in the evaluation between different people will be levelled. Some will find everything fantastic no matter how bad it is and some will find a hair in every bowl of soup. On an aggregate level the evaluation achieves a fair assessment.

Customers will give you first-hand, up-to-date information at very low cost

This structured feedback that can be rendered instantly into numbers helps users benefit from content generated in multiple languages. It helps the travel agent to identify problem areas quickly without having to read through all emails. And it helps all users select a new hotel more quickly because the information could also be used as selection criteria when searching for a holiday destination.

Without structured user-generated content the customer might, for example, look for a hotel with a golf course and childcare facilities that costs no more than $1,200 for a week for two adults and a child, including all meals. This is all information that can be provided by the travel agent without having to rely on user-generated content. However, the web site might be searchable only by price. The customer would now have to look at the particulars of every single hotel or resort, which might be several hundred or thousand hotels, to find one that met the other criteria, and they may not have any numerical ratings.

If structured user-generated content is available, however, the user can further narrow down the choices by also asking for a hotel that has an average user rating of a minimum of 5 points for childcare and a minimum of 4 points for food. The travel agent web site would then come back with a greatly reduced list of hotels that fulfil these criteria. It would also display the number of respondents that the rating is based on. Obviously it is more reliable if a rating of 5 for childcare is based on 200 users than if it is based on only two.

Feedback from the customers, therefore, actually becomes the basis for more value-added information and thus for further customization. If the customer relied on that information when he chose his hotel he will see the benefit of it and therefore be more willing to answer a well-conceived question list when evaluating the hotel later himself.

In order to make the web site really useful it has to display all user feedback that is mailed, except for offensive language or comments that have nothing to do with the site's primary criteria. In that case the customer should receive an email stating the reasons why his feedback has not been posted. Displaying honest – both good and bad – customer feedback on the web site gives the retailer credibility, which is extremely important in the impersonal Internet environment. For example, Amazon.com is not afraid of displaying negative comments; every comment is always couched as a reader's personal opinion. The more customer feedback there is, the easier it is for a new customer to make an informed decision; this, in turn, increases customer satisfaction and, ultimately, customer retention.

Be sure always either to display the comment on the site or to let the customer know why it has not been displayed because people will test you. Some people might send in negative comments just to check if you will actually display them. If you do not, the web site loses its credibility because the customer will suspect that all other comments have also been screened or edited. News travels fast in the times of the Internet, and bad news travels even faster. A web site that has not displayed one customer's comment might quickly find itself in an unenviable position where the credibility of the whole site is being questioned in news groups and the press.

News travels fast in the times of the Internet, and bad news travels even faster

As always with user-generated content there is the danger that some people will try to abuse the system. A hotel chain might hire some college students to do nothing but submit favourable comments to the different travel agent web sites about hotels of that group. Or even worse, unfavourable comments about competitors' hotels. Depending on the amount of time these people spend generating messages they could actually distort the rating of a hotel. The web site, therefore, has to find mechanisms to control these activities, because they will ruin the value of the user-generated content and undermine the value proposition of the web site.

In the case of eBay, only users who have actually auctioned an item or bought at auction may comment about the trading partner. As we discussed earlier, this still leaves room for fraud, but the time and energy involved in carrying out a scam are so great that it is probably not worth it. Amazon could ensure that only people who have actually bought a particular book on Amazon will be able to write a comment on that book. This would limit the user-generated content, of course, because people who have bought the book elsewhere or got it as a gift through someone else who bought it at Amazon will not be able to comment on the book.

This might be the reason why Amazon allows anybody to comment on any book they wish, whether they bought it at Amazon or not. You have to ask yourself, however, what the payoff is for someone who tries to perpetrate a scam. Are a few friendly reviews from acquaintances of the author really a problem? Probably not, compared to the damage you can do by trying to exclude them, because participation is part of the Amazon idea.

Participation is part of the Amazon idea

Travel agent restrictions make more sense. They could easily make sure that only people who have actually booked a particular hotel through the web site will be able to comment on it. Those measures cannot fully exclude fraud but make it much more difficult. And, of course, there is always the threat that any hotel group that is caught contributing falsified customer feedback will be excluded from online sales for a certain time, which can mean significant revenue losses once the online bookings constitute a significant share of the total market. It would also lead to negative publicity that would probably hurt the company even more than the revenue loss by seriously damaging the corporate identity.

Apart from publicizing customer comments and opinions for the benefit of the customer, such feedback is also invaluable for the online retailer himself. It gives the retailer a chance to improve his products and service. Through customer feedback, the retailer can easily identify those products that sound good on the web site – otherwise, customers would not have bought them in the first place – but fail to satisfy customers. Such products should be improved or eliminated because they lead to customer defection and negative word of mouth. This is intrinsic to the customization model we discussed in the Introduction, a model that was lost for so long with the advent of mass production and the wider markets permitted by modern transportation.

To obtain the full benefit of customer feedback the web site should also offer an option for commenting not only on product and service quality but also on the processes of the company, such as the distribution and payment systems. Customer feedback gives the retailer a chance to obtain immediate information about the efficiency of his company. This kind of information is not meant to be publicized on the web site but serves as fast and efficient intelligence for the retailer and should be looked at as an early warning system. It is absolutely the fastest and least expensive way for the retailer to find out if some processes within his value chain are not working properly. This is especially valuable if those parts of the value chain are outsourced to other companies. It would take the retailer considerable time to find out that something was not working properly if there were no customer feedback.

Another type of user content is generated by the customers but mainly without intention to publicize. It happens that in the process of choosing custom product features, customers can create product specifications or designs that are unique and interesting enough to appeal to other customers. These designs can also be made available to other users, with the consent of the customers who generated the design. These options are discussed in detail later in this volume.

Direct communication between users

In addition to communication between the customer and the retailer that is made available to all customers, there is also the possibility that two customers can communicate directly with each other. Direct communication between users increases the value of the web site for other users and gives the individual user the feeling of being part of a community. Such communication can take place via bulletin boards, where one user posts a message for other users who read it later, or it can take place in online chat forums where both customers are actually online at the same time. New technology can allow customers to see who else is online and to communicate instantly with them.

> **Direct communication between users increases the value of the web site for other users and gives the individual user the feeling of being part of a community**

Many companies find this communication between users to be extremely valuable. Providing a forum and monitoring the activity is actually just another way to provide value-added information. Imagine a customer who is trying to select a hotel for an upcoming holiday. The customer basically wants a golf hotel but is also very keen on in line skating; therefore, she would like to know if the roads around the hotel are suitable for skating on. The information is not available in the travel agent's hotel description; other customers have not commented on the state of traffic and road surfaces. So the customer could post an enquiry at the bulletin board of the travel agent asking other customers if they can answer the question. This could either be people who have been to the same hotel and, while they might not skate themselves, can still answer the question, or it could be residents who live near the hotel and also surf the same web site to book their holidays.

The web site ***www.lonelyplanet.com*** offers a bulletin board called 'The Thorn Tree' where travellers can post individual questions regarding their next travel plans. Usually at least two to four people post answers within the first 48 hours of posting. While Lonely Planet is not a travel agent but a travel book publisher, a very similar site could also be imagined for travel agents. While Lonely Planet user communication serves to build the community on the web site and as a marketing tool for Lonely Planet's books, for a travel agent the communication between users could be direct value-added information for bookings.

virtual visit

Another interesting option presents itself if the number of people who surf a particular web site is large enough at any given point in time. Instead of posting the question on a bulletin board and having to come back two days later to check for the answers, real-time messaging between different customers could be possible. Imagine our customer again who is searching for a holiday hotel and has some particular questions that the web site and the user-generated feedback cannot answer. She could then pose an online question. The web site would quickly check if there are any other users online who have already been to the hotel in question. Those users would receive a note on their screen, asking them if they would be prepared to answer a question from another user who is currently online and wants to go to the same hotel. If the customers agree, real-time messaging between those users would be possible on the web site.

It becomes more and more difficult for other web sites to attract new customers if they do not have the necessary number of users to be able to offer real-time messaging

To go a step further: when a certain hotel is selected, the web site could immediately show how many other users are currently online who have already been to that hotel in case the new customer has any questions. For real-time messaging between users to work a considerable critical mass will be necessary to find at least a few people online for every hotel offered at any point in time. Once a travel agent web site has reached this critical mass however, it becomes immediately much more valuable for other users. The law of increasing returns takes hold and accelerates the growth of the user community on this web site. It becomes more and more difficult for other web sites to attract new customers if they do not have the necessary number of users to be able to offer real-time messaging.

Once real-time messaging between users becomes a value-added, commonly known feature of the web site that also attracts new users, the willingness of these new users to answer questions themselves is also bound to rise. If customers have themselves already received valuable information through real-time messaging with other users they are more likely to be open to answering questions.

One of the preconditions for offering a focused real-time messaging option is to identify any user online as soon as they log on. If you only know that you have currently 15,000 people online but have no idea whether they have already booked to travel through you and to which hotel, focused real-time messaging is not possible. It will not be received very favourably by the 15,000 people if they all get a message box on their screen asking them to provide information on a particular hotel if they can. It is likely that 14,995 of the users will never have been to that particular hotel and will find the message very annoying. In addition, you would have to send all information requests to all users who are currently online, which would mean the screen would be nothing but non-stop requests. The site would quickly lose its appeal.

So in order to offer focused real-time messaging between users it is crucial to identify repeat customers, the only ones who can reliably answer questions, as soon as they enter the web site. Once easy-to-use real-time messaging between users becomes a well-known and highly valued feature of the web site, users will be more likely to identify themselves at the beginning of a session.

In addition to the direct benefits of being able to make more informed decisions about particular hotels, the customer also feels part of the larger web site community. Even better, customer loyalty actually increases, because that customer cannot take the web site community with her when she chooses to shop at a competitor's web site.

Another example of a community that lives on user-generated content is Silicon Investor (**www.techstocks.com**). It is basically a financial discussion site. People can become members of Silicon Investor free of charge and start their own bulletin board. There are discussion groups for most traded stocks where people will discuss their opinions and information related to that stock. Many posted messages also contain links to other web sites where more information on the particular stock can be found. Or people will insert press clippings on the particular company. This can be especially valuable if you are interested in stocks that are trading in another country. A particular piece of information about the Commonwealth Bank of Australia will not necessarily make the news in Paris. If you hold that stock, however, you might be very grateful if a participant of Silicon Investor in Australia keeps you up to date with the latest developments.

> **It is like looking at one piece of a 1,000-piece jigsaw puzzle that happens to be black and white, trying to figure out from that if you are trying to construct the picture of a zebra, a skyscraper or a fashion model's dress**

Silicon Investor is not validated and accurate information; it is many opinions and little nuggets of information. It is a bit like a puzzle where you do not have all the parts, and might even have some wrong parts, but you still have enough to get an idea of the whole picture. One person might have talked to a sales rep of the company in question in Singapore and found out that the new product that has just been launched worldwide has exceeded all sales expectations in the Asian market within the first week. Another might have heard from her lawyer brother in New York who represents the company that it is desperately searching for experts to start up a new business in a specific sector. The third contributor might have been driving by the company plant in Manchester and seen that the company had introduced a third shift on weekends to keep up with the rise in demand, since all the lights were on in the factory on Saturday.

Each of these pieces by itself might not be worth much. It is like looking at one piece of a 1,000-piece jigsaw puzzle that happens to be black and white, trying to figure out from that if

virtual visit

121

you are trying to construct the picture of a zebra, a skyscraper or a fashion model's dress. One little piece by itself is worthless. By the time you have accumulated 100 pieces the information might become very valuable, however, because you might be able to guess the whole picture. You can, of course, also wait until you have all 1,000 pieces in order to be sure to recognize the full picture correctly. Unfortunately, by that time, the information is totally worthless for stock speculation because everyone else also sees the whole picture and market prices have adjusted accordingly.

User-generated content never has any guarantee that the information is accurate

Since stockmarket speculation is based on knowing something before everyone else knows it, the Silicon Investor web site is also a great source for rumours, of course, and investors are anxious to believe them – frequently too anxious. If you have been part of the Silicon Investor community and have followed the discussion groups for some time, you might be able to tell which of the other members have good information and which ones do not. Some always seem to be better informed or make the right guesses, so other people will start to listen to their comments.

There is, of course, a high likelihood of people trying to influence prices by introducing wrong information. As always with user-generated content Silicon Investor as a discussion site does not try to validate comments or opinions but makes it very clear that the contributions are the opinion of individuals. User-generated content never has any guarantee that the information is accurate. It is always only the personal opinion of another customer. All web sites using user-generated content should make it quite clear that it lies in the basis of user-generated content that the web site cannot take any responsibility for what is generated by users in this context.

Apart from generating a community on the web site and using value-added information to enhance customer loyalty, there are also considerable potential savings when participants answer other users' questions on the company's products. Either the question would remain unanswered if it were not for the users or the question would end up in the company's call centre where it would generate considerable costs.

Chapter 13

Loyalty programmes

A loyalty programme is a way of influencing and changing a customer's buying behaviour. Generally, retailers tend to reward customers for desired behaviour that leads to greater sales volume, increased revenues, higher profits or other dividends, including referrals of new customers. The best way of obtaining loyal customers, however, is to offer great service, value-added information, customization and user-generated content. Everything we

A loyalty programme is a way of influencing and changing a customer's buying behaviour

have discussed so far is in some senses nothing but one big customer loyalty scheme. Nevertheless, there are certain features of loyalty programmes that can enhance even web sites that are already extremely sophisticated.

Customer loyalty schemes are generally not very well suited for generating new traffic or converting spectators into customers. They are, however, great incentives to get customers back to your site, increasing the share of wallet and the profitability of these customers. Loyalty programmes have to be adapted to the web site's particular business. There are two major things that have to be designed when starting a customer loyalty programme. First, you have to decide which customer activities you want to foster. Second, you have to decide which rewards are most interesting for the customers you particularly value.

Rewarded customer activities

With any loyalty programme there are several different options for choosing the customer activities to encourage: a reward can be used to create incentives for first-time use of a new product or service, to refer new customers to the site or just to generate revenue or enhance profitability.

First-time use

Loyalty schemes can offer incentives for tasks that overcome reluctance to buy. Doing something for the first time often constitutes a barrier for a customer because he must obtain and understand new information, gain trust for a new retailer and generally do things he has never done before. One way to make sure the customer is not put off by the barriers is to offer high loyalty incentives for doing something.

Loyalty schemes can offer incentives for tasks that overcome reluctance to buy

For example, if the retailer introduces a new payment system, he could offer a large loyalty bonus for any first-time user. Similarly, the introduction of new telephone cards could be linked to a bonus for the first call using the new card. Once the customer has cleared the first-time user hurdle and has discovered how easy and convenient it (hopefully) really is, chances are he will use the card more often, thus increasing the revenue for the retailer. When offering first-time bonuses, the retailer must be able to identify the customer correctly; otherwise, repeat customers will claim the first-time bonus every single time using slightly different names. This can be avoided not by giving a direct incentive, but by offering points in a loyalty programme in which the customer must accumulate points before gaining rewards.

Another example of this kind of incentive is Lufthansa (***www.lufthansa.com***). Lufthansa sent an email to all members of its frequent flier programme who were online and asked them to register for the online distribution of their mile account statements. As an incentive they offered 5,000 bonus miles for everyone who became part of the programme before a certain date. If you received the online version for a trial period and later decided that you preferred the paper versions of the account statements, you could easily change back to paper in your personal profile on the web site. But chances are that even those people who only changed to the online version in order to get the 5,000 bonus miles will stick with it once they have tried it out. The benefits to Lufthansa are clear. Apart from attracting customers to its web site with the chance of selling flights directly and without having to pay travel agent fees there are, of course, also considerable direct savings involved: printing and mailing costs for the account statements are significantly reduced, for instance.

Lufthansa used the same method of incentive when it introduced electronic tickets and automated check-in at airports. For the first couple of months the use of these new devices was always associated with frequent traveller miles for each use. Once people became used to the new system, the bonus was dropped.

Referred new customers

Another valuable web site feature entails giving incentives to loyal customers who tell their friends or colleagues how wonderful the web site is. This is an online variation of 'word of mouth'. Loyal customers can be offered the opportunity to send an email to a friend with a personal message and a link to the web site. This digitized 'word of mouse' testimonial also allows the retailer to reward the most active advocates of his web site within the customer loyalty scheme. If it normally costs a retailer $200 to obtain a new customer, he can easily offer quite a high bonus for a successful referral, especially since referred customers tend to be more loyal than customers obtained in any other way.

This digitized 'word of mouse' testimonial also allows the retailer to reward the most active advocates of his web site within the customer loyalty scheme

A word of caution! It is important to let the customer know that your site is personalized, especially when word of mouth is an important avenue for obtaining new customers. If the site has been actively customized by the customer herself, she knows of other options that the web site could offer and can therefore also judge for herself if other features that she is not using might be interesting for a friend or colleague. If the customization was basically passive, however, the customer might not realize that customization has taken place at all. Normally this does not matter. The customer does not even have to know. It is enough if she is happy with the way the product or service is presented. In the case of a loyalty scheme that is built on referring new people the customer might come to the mistaken conclusion that the web site would not be of interest to any of her friends because she does not realize that it has actually been customized to her individual needs. She may like the site but may not advocate it to friends or colleagues with different interests. If you want to base your customer loyalty programmes on referred customers and have based your web site heavily on passive customization, it is imperative to let the customer know that customization has taken place to get the full benefit of the customer loyalty programmes.

A variation of this loyalty option is the affiliate programme. Take the example of Network Solutions (***www.nsi.com***). This company is in the business of web address registration and is one of the global registrars of the top-level domains, including .com, .net, .org and .edu. Since more and more private customers also register their own domains, Network Solutions offers an affiliate programme for private customers besides its affiliate programme for Internet service providers. The affiliate programme provides an easy way for companies or individuals to establish a link to Network Solutions' web address registration and other products from its web sites, enabling them to earn additional revenue and add value for their web site visitors.

For example, the fact that Mr Paul Duffney has registered his own domain and his friends can now reach him under Paul@Duffney.com does not mean that he now wants to enter the business of selling domain names. It just means that it will be easier for them to remember how to reach him, instead of the awkward pdufn12@mw.lgd-ni.dbpsm.com that he used as a mailing address before. Furthermore, it has become a status symbol to have your own domain. And again, chances are that most of Paul's friends did not even know that it is possible for private individuals to buy their own domain and are now also thinking about getting one. And what could be easier than going to the web site of your friend, clicking on the affiliate logo and registering your own domain? Therefore, it makes a lot of sense for NSI to offer such a programme. As a referral bonus they offer a minimum of ten per cent of each sale that is generated through a referral, which means if you get ten of your friends to buy their own domain through your new web site, your own domain is free.

It has become a status symbol to have your own domain

In the business-to-business world customer loyalty and referral schemes might even be introduced on a two-way basis. Network Solutions has established an alliance programme that enables Network Solutions and participating companies to provide reciprocal distribution channels for each other's complementary services.

In the world of the Internet it is fairly easy to track how much revenue the referred customer has generated or how profitable he is if the underlying database has been set up to support those features. Therefore, instead of rewarding users for referred customers, as in the bricks and mortar loyalty programmes, it becomes easy actually to reward revenue or profitability of the new customer instead. This makes the programme an even more powerful tool for the retailer because it means he is only rewarding actions that have actually generated revenue or profit for him.

What could be easier than going to the web site of your friend, clicking on the affiliate logo and registering your own domain?

Revenue and profitability

A loyalty programme is also a powerful way of influencing and changing customer buying behaviour. The retailer increases his share of wallet and profitability by rewarding certain customer behaviour. In existing loyalty programmes retailers usually reward the revenue of the customer. Once all information about the customers' buying behaviour is digitized it should not be too difficult to reward customer profitability as well. When rewarding revenue there is always the danger of rewarding behaviour that in reality decreases profitability. When you set up your customer loyalty programme to reward profitability directly there is no doubt.

To calculate customer profitability you have to know what products or services a customer buys at what price, how profitable those services are for you and what the costs of service are for that particular customer. So even if two customers buy the same amount of a particular product they might differ in profitability because one customer continually writes lengthy emails to the customer service centre that take time to be answered whereas the other customer requires no additional service.

In the business-to-business world customer loyalty and referral schemes might even be introduced on a two-way basis

For most bricks and mortar companies calculating customer profitability is still an illusion. The majority of companies struggle when they are trying to determine how many individual customers they actually have. They struggle even more when they have to find out the revenue from each. Asked about the profitability for their different products most companies only have a rough idea, which might not even remotely correspond to the facts, and cost to serve the individual customer is even further away for most. Since all information and customer interaction is digitized on the Internet, it becomes easier for the retailer to obtain all the pertinent information and to consolidate it under one customer account number. As soon as the customer is identified every action he takes will count towards his total profitability.

Apart from the number of purchases and the number of service emails, the retailer can also take into account how many new customers have been referred, their profitability, and overall contributions of user-generated content to the site. Everything else being equal, a customer who regularly contributes content to the site is worth more than someone else who buys just as much but keeps silent. The online market research capabilities are an important feature. As we will discuss later, you will even know which suggestions for new products come from your most loyal and most profitable customers and might therefore have top priority.

> **When rewarding revenue there is always the danger of rewarding behaviour that in reality decreases profitability**

Most customer loyalty programmes are currently set up as an add-on activity. They are run by a different department of the company working on add-on systems and often do not even have customer purchase information readily available. If you want to reap the full benefits of the customer loyalty programme in online commerce it has to be integrated with every process of the company: communication with the customer, service level, the product design and even the pricing strategy for that customer, which we also discuss in a later chapter.

Loyalty programmes are much easier to administer on the Internet than traditional loyalty programmes because purchase information is already available in a digitized format. Therefore, such programmes require less administrative upkeep, once the underlying database is installed and integrated with the work flow system.

> **Everything else being equal, a customer who regularly contributes content to the site is worth more than someone else who buys just as much but keeps silent**

Correctly measuring customer profitability online is not easy and it should not be underestimated. Even though all information might be available in a digitized format, this does not mean that it can also be analyzed in a timely manner. If you want to build customization on the basis of customer loyalty and profitability, customer profitability information must not take months to calculate and consolidate. You need the information online, within a split second of the customer logging on.

That functionality has to be integrated into the underlying database from the start: programming such functionality as an add-on to an already existing system does not work. But the effort is worth it because it gives you possibilities for fine-tuning your interaction with the customer that other companies can only dream about. The advantages when you can actually reward customer profitability are obvious. You can focus your rewards and your whole customization programme on those people who really make a difference to your bottom line.

As mentioned before, most companies are pretty far away from being able to use customer profitability as a measure for rewarding customer loyalty. But even properly using customer revenue information can yield high rewards. American Express is a good example of how a bricks and mortar company can use loyalty programmes to increase the share of wallet by rewarding revenue. When credit cards started to become popular, issuing companies could increase their revenue by increasing the number of cardholders and the number of shops that would accept the card. However, those two marketing options have been almost fully exploited. Nowadays most people have several credit or charge cards. Issuing another card increases the number of cardholders but not necessarily the amount charged to the individual card. At the same time most shops will accept all major credit cards and, logically, shop owners usually have a clear preference for accepting cards that charge the lowest commission – not Amex's traditional strength. The only reason they accept cards that charge higher commission at all is because customers continuously want to use them.

So the decision about which card is used is up to the customer – the moment he walks up to the cash register is key. So how do you make sure that he puts your card on the counter and not a competitor's? Faced with that question, American Express developed a customer loyalty programme that is intended to shift the customer's preferences towards using the Amex card. For every dollar charged to the card the customer receives loyalty points, which can be accumulated and then used for flights and hotels and discount merchandise as loyalty incentives. American Express can pay for these incentives by charging a higher commission for their card. But since the commission is paid by the seller and not by the buyer, the total price for the customer remains the same. Therefore it is a useful tool to shift customer preferences towards a certain card and generate revenue for the credit card company.

Types of customer incentive

Now that we have looked at the different customer activities that a loyalty programme could encourage we will have a look at the different incentives you can give to your customers to influence their behaviour. The kinds of incentives that your customers will actually respond to depend very much on the characteristics of those customers. Therefore customer loyalty incentives have the greatest effect if they are also customized.

Luckily, by now you should have accumulated so much knowledge about your customer through all the transactions you have done with her, that it should be fairly easy selecting rewards that will actually be viewed as an incentive utilizing methods of passive customization. However, once more, active customization is a better method than passive customization. If you offer different options people can choose whatever is most important for them.

The mention of customer loyalty rewards makes most people immediately think of receiving something for free. But that is only one possibility. You can offer anything from preferred treatment to free additional service to information that is not available to the average customer.

The mention of customer loyalty rewards makes most people immediately think of receiving something for free. But that is only one possibility

The important thing is that incentives be perceived as such by the customer. Incentives that work perfectly well for frequent travellers could be a total failure for an online grocery store. Even within one company different kinds of customers might go for different incentives. For the occasional traveller who has accumulated a certain number of points with an airline, a free flight for her and her partner to an attractive weekend location might be a great incentive. Someone who flies 200,000 miles a year usually does not get too excited about another free flight. Their idea of fun may be not spending the weekend on a plane. Not surprisingly, the most successful loyalty programmes offer a whole range of different rewards that allow the customer to select those that are of highest value to him. We now take a look at different types of possible incentives.

Free products

Not surprisingly, the most successful loyalty programmes offer a whole range of different rewards that allow the customer to select those that are of highest value to him

The most common rewards that people think of when they think about rewarding customers are free products. The old slogan 'Buy ten, get one free' has lost none of its magic. But free offers can also include things that are otherwise not available or are hard to get. Airlines have been very successful with an offer of an hour of pilot training in a full flight simulator as an adventure bonus for heavy business travellers.

American Express's loyalty programme has become so extensive that it has almost become a second currency, offering everything from airline flights, hotel vouchers, newspaper subscriptions, concert tickets and wine. Chances are that in such a wide variety of rewards every member of the programme will find an incentive that is personally rewarding. Giving financial rewards to your most loyal or profitable customers can even mean having individual pricing. We will have a closer look at the possibilities of customer loyalty price differentiation in a later chapter.

Free additional service

Loyalty programmes in many cases become an issue of redistributing money between employers and employees. The possibility of this kind of redistribution plays an important role in designing incentives. The company selling the products and services always has to know who its target customer is.

Frequent flier programmes are the primary case in point. The individual spends company money to travel but by specifying a particular airline he personally receives the reward instead of refunding it to the company. For these customers it makes little sense to offer flights at a lower price in return for their customer status because they do not individually profit. Carriers therefore have to explore additional incentives, such as telephone check-in, or free upgrades on long-distance flights. If someone flies regularly with a certain airline and his company only allows him to book economy class, he might be very interested in upgrades to business class for long flights. If he knows that you will upgrade him on long-distance flights he is also likely to use your airline for shorter trips.

Free additional service can include a wide variety of things. A seller of technical appliances could offer a warranty extension of 12 months for his most loyal customers. A grocery retailer could offer free delivery. A travel agent can allow good customers to change their holiday bookings at the last minute without a fee. This can be especially interesting for customers who often have to change their holiday plans at short notice for work-related reasons. The most profitable customers could even be offered more bonus points per purchase than regular customers.

Preferred treatment

All incentives described so far lead to higher costs of service because the company has to pay for the free products or the free additional service. Preferred treatment is different because it entails the redistribution of scarce resources rather than subsidizing special activity. Preferred treatment means that the company will give scarce resources to their most loyal and most profitable customers.

One does not expect to find a lot of problems associated with scarce resources in a free market economy, because one would expect the market to solve the shortfall immediately.

However, a closer look reveals quite a few shortages that cannot easily be overcome without high investment and reducing the profitability of the company.

Any service associated with using available capacity can easily become scarce for a limited period of time. The best example is the number of seats in a particular plane. A certain number of seats are available on the 7 o'clock aircraft from London to Paris and if those are all taken, the resource becomes scarce. It is still much more profitable for the airline to leave a few customers unsatisfied than to use a second aircraft to live up to the demand. But if you leave a few customers unsatisfied, you had better make sure that it is not your most profitable customers that go away in anger. Some airlines even offer a guarantee to their most loyal customers that they will get a seat on any flight if they book within 24 hours before the departure, no matter for how long that flight has already been fully booked.

> **Any service associated with both certain service capacity and varying demand can become scarce on short notice and is therefore a good lever for preferred treatment for the most loyal or most profitable customers**

Basically, any service associated with both certain service capacity and varying demand can become scarce on short notice and is therefore a good lever for preferred treatment for the most loyal or most profitable customers. The possible variants are almost without limit. Imagine that you run a hotel. You need a certain time between the check-out of one customer and the check-in of another in order to make up the room. Making up an individual room is probably not going to take more than half an hour. Nevertheless most hotels require at least four hours between their regular check-out time and their check-in time because they do not have the necessary staff to make up all of the hotel's rooms within 30 minutes. For their most loyal customers, however, they can offer a special late check-out or early check-in. Even among the loyal customers the company is able to distinguish between different levels of status.

> **Recognize also that the customer does not even have to know that he is included in a loyalty scheme**

In the online world possibilities for preferred treatment can include faster or more personal response to emails. When a customer sends an email to the company via the web site there are scarce resources to be allocated, since the employees cannot answer all mails at the same time. So when the customer identifies himself before sending a mail, the work flow management system of the web site can ensure that the mails of the most loyal or most profitable customers show up first and are consequently answered first.

This is similar to giving different telephone numbers to loyal customers to reach the call centre with shorter or no waiting times. Note that loyalty schemes also offer incentives for the customer to identify himself, because only then will he be able to get the full benefit of the loyalty scheme. This early identification in turn helps to make customization possible.

Recognize also that the customer does not even have to know he is included in a loyalty scheme. Since the Internet provides a unique opportunity to market to segments of one, retailers actually can reward extremely loyal or profitable customers by offering them products at a very special price available to no one else. Even if legal obligations in some countries require the retailer to offer the product to everyone for that price, this does not mean that he must actively inform everyone about it. Thus, the retailer can favour highly desirable customers by giving them first-hand information about specials.

If you differentiate between customers based on their profitability, chances are that you will get higher returns than by treating everyone the same

Even if the customer knows you have a loyalty scheme he does not have to know you are actually measuring profitability instead of revenue. You might not want to communicate to the customer, and to your competitors, what profitability is associated with which products. But you can still use profitability internally. The customer does not have to know that he is one of your most profitable and most loyal customers. He only has to know that he gets superb service, never has to wait to get through by telephone, always receives prompt replies to emails, and gets product offers that are customized to his needs at a great price.

Of course, it would be nice if you could offer this kind of service to every single customer. But the economics work against it. If you differentiate between customers based on their profitability, chances are that you will get higher returns than by treating everyone the same. That is the whole principle of customer loyalty programmes. If there is a certain status associated with the loyalty programme, it can be very helpful for retailers to inform customers of a loyalty scheme: knowing that he has attained a certain status with a retailer, and may therefore be accorded valuable privileges and exclusive treatment, can be a very powerful incentive for a customer to be loyal to a web site.

Part V

Customized production

Chapter 14

Demand for customized products

Stepping back in time again to look at the development of products and services, we see that the number of customized products declined steadily after the beginning of the Industrial Revolution and the development of mass production, although their absolute number and sophistication increased beyond all dreams. Before the beginning of industrialization, basically all products were built by hand to one degree or another. Even those that were cast from reusable moulds were customized by human fallibility, at the very least.

In the early stages of mass production, the individual needs and desires of the users were subordinated to the necessities of a uniform production process. Since then, the pendulum has slowly been swinging back towards customization. Manufacturers have started to produce more and more variants of the same product in order to fulfil the needs of individual customers. Current trends in consumer behaviour and preferences indicate that this development is likely to continue and even accelerate. In today's buyer's markets, customers are becoming more assertive and want their specific needs to be satisfied at an acceptable price.

> **With the emergence of the Internet, companies can now produce for the world market and still communicate with every single customer**

Manufacturers, however, are still cut off from customers by powerful retail chains and distribution networks. With the emergence of the Internet, companies can now produce for the world market and still communicate with every single customer. The Internet offers a fast and inexpensive communication medium for detailed information which makes customization possible to an extent previously unthinkable. The Internet and available production technology combine two advantages. They allow companies to reap the cost advantages of mass production, while at the same time companies can also reap the benefits of high customer satisfaction through customized production. This includes products and services in both the business-to-business and the business-to-consumer areas. Examples of customized products available on the web today include consumer goods such as skis, shoes, bicycles and books as well as business-to-business products such as scales, windows and chemicals.

Mass customization

What are the unique advantages of the Internet for customizing products? Does it mean we will go back to an age of bespoke suits and built-to-order furniture? No. The goal is not to go back to the totally individual, made-to-order products as we had before the Industrial Revolution, only this time for the mass market. In the old days, true customization was a privilege only for the few. To replicate that for the mass market would be prohibitively expensive. The trick is to combine the advantages of mass production, such as economy, continuity, and stability of the production processes, with attention to the tastes and service requirements of individual customers.

> **The trick is to combine the advantages of mass production with attention to the tastes and service requirements of individual customers**

The result is called mass customization. Products are not one of a kind, but, generally speaking, assembled to order for the individual customer from mass-produced components. Probably one of the best-known examples is Dell Computers. There is no standard Dell PC, although the whole production chain and final assembly are highly standardized. However, the resulting computers are totally individual. Dell showed the world that custom-made PCs need neither be more expensive than mass-produced PCs nor have longer delivery times.

When considering the potential for customized production, you have to look at two things. The first consideration is who would be interested in buying a customized version of your product. Customization has to represent a distinct competitive advantage over standardized competitors or else you will not sell a thing. We will have a look at different competitive advantages for mass customization later.

After you have identified a demand for customized products you have to look at the supply side (see chapter 16). The critical questions here are what characteristics of the product and the production process lend themselves to customization. Direct communication with the customer via the Internet allows a company to recognize and analyze patterns of customer demand as well as facilitating choices about the production process.

It should also be mentioned that in some cases the line between customized communication and customized production can be somewhat arbitrary. In the case of online newspapers, for example, the communication on the web site is simultaneous with the sale.

Growth of demand

The growing demand for customized products is undeniable. We have come a long way from the first days of mass production where the most important consideration for product design was whether it lent itself to an unchanging assembly line. For most products today the customer can choose from a great number of variations of the same product produced by competing companies. Even with mass production it is possible to produce a vast number of variations.

Internet retail is not limited by shelf space in a single location and can therefore offer an incredible variety of different products

One of the most striking differences between bricks and mortar retail and Internet retail is that Internet retail is not limited by shelf space in a single location and can therefore offer an incredible variety of different products. Internet book retailers, for example, can present millions of different books on their web sites compared to several hundred thousand at even the very largest traditional bookshops. Therefore bricks and mortar book retailers focus on the more recent releases that are likely to sell fastest. Internet bookshops, however, can also offer the whole backlist at very little extra cost, a distinct competitive advantage.

Of course, books, whether they are sold in traditional bookshops or on the Internet, are the same. They are generally not customized. For mass-customized products, however, the value for the customer is not greater choice but to be able quickly to define the product he wants, get it produced to his needs, and buy it.

Take clothing, for example. Do you remember when you last met someone who was wearing exactly the same clothes as you? It probably happens very rarely although the great majority of clothes are mass produced. The number of variations is so large that the chance you will actually meet someone wearing exactly the same design and fabric as you is extremely slim. So one might think that with the vast variety available consumers would be content.

> **For mass-customized products, the value for the customer is not greater choice, but to be able quickly to define the product he wants, get it produced to his needs, and buy it**

But the reality of the matter seems to be just the opposite. Near infinite variety does not necessarily equate with high customer satisfaction. When I want to buy a new dark grey suit I do not actually want 500 dark grey suits to choose from. Things are made even worse if there are 5,000 different dark grey suits instead of 500. As a matter of fact, I want just one dark grey suit that fits me. Just one suit. Forget the other 499 or 4,999! And if I can get that one suit without searching and trying them all on, that is great added convenience for me.

So far most manufacturers have tried to solve the problem of differing customer preferences by designing and stocking more and more variations. The more variations you have and the more rapidly consumer preferences change the bigger your eventual inventory problems. You might end up with thousands of products in stock that no one wants and still not be able to fulfil the demand for a few other products that are out of stock.

Basically your whole company is at the mercy of fickle customer desires. You depend on being able to predict consumer behaviour down to a great level of detail for every single one of your products. The clothing industry shows how difficult this can be. You might have your whole store and warehouse overflowing with different clothes and many customers will still not find what they want. They might like the cut of the dress but not the colour, or they may like both, but not the fabric. If they finally find something perfect, it may not be available in their size. As a consequence a considerable number of clothes have to be discounted radically in order to sell at all.

All this happens because you produce something without actually knowing what the customer wants. Some companies have tried to address the problem. Benetton, for example, tries to reduce the problem of quick shifts in customer taste by colouring clothes at the very last stage in the production process to capitalize on the latest trend. This cuts down on stocks and reduces risk by cutting down the time period over which it has to forecast, but it does not address the root cause of the problem.

Your whole company is at the mercy of fickle customer desires

Mass customization combined with the Internet becomes economically feasible on a large scale. Any development of a new strategy or idea for a new business, product or service however should always start from the customer perspective and mass customization is no exception. That is why we will consider the customer perspective first.

Why do customers buy customized products or services? There are many reasons. They may be looking for a product functionality that fulfils their desires or requirements. Or they may want added convenience; instead of selecting from a variety of different products, they can directly get what they want. Status and entertainment can also be important reasons for buying customized products. Some people enjoy designing customized products themselves and enjoy the attention they attract. And, last but not least, the price can be a consideration for customers since customized products can actually be cheaper than mass-produced products.

Major drivers of demand

In the business-to-business market the major drivers for customer behaviour are more likely to be functionality and price than status or fun. Whatever the market, however, it is unlikely that all reasons will apply to all customers. As always one of the most important things when designing a new business is to have a clear picture of target customer groups and to match those customers with the various reasons. While we cannot do this matching for you definitively, we can outline the basic reasons and the concepts behind them.

Product functionality

The most obvious reason to buy a customized product is because it actually meets the user's requirements fully without any compromises. The suit fits. Mass customization does not mean producing infinite variety to meet every last customer idiosyncrasy. The cost would far outweigh any benefit to the bulk of customers. The choices have to be valuable and meaningful. Endless variation increases the number of choices but the value added does not justify the extra costs. So one of the most important criteria for mass customization is to offer variations of product functionality that are actually important for the customers in your target group.

In the business-to-business market the major drivers for customer behaviour are more likely to be functionality and price than status or fun

Imagine a company selling custom-made shirts. The basic variables could include sleeve length, body length and collar circumference from measurements supplied by the customer, targeting customers with body shapes that do not fit the norm, as well as the status conscious who like the idea of wearing customer-made clothing. Options that can be selected on the web site could also include fancy collar forms, designer buttons or cuff links, extravagant colours and cloth designs, targeting fashion conscious customers. As we will see later, real-time market research based on the choices customers make among these variables can be a great help in finding out what is really important for your customer group.

Customization involves not only products; it can also be extended to service associated with the product. This might include an individually printed user manual. Instead of getting a user manual in ten different languages describing all variants of the product, the customer would get one in the selected language describing only those product features that are actually included in the product he has selected. He could even select a manual for experts, which explains all features concisely but in technical terminology, or one for the lay person that would describe the features in plain English, or whichever language he has chosen, and not drift into technical detail.

When you start designing a customized product make sure to include the whole customer buying experience and also think about customizing service options

Other services could also be customized. The customer could choose to have the product delivered and assembled, or pick it up and install it himself. He could also opt for either a basic warranty or an extended service contract. When you start designing a customized product make sure to include the whole customer buying experience and also think about customizing service options.

Added convenience

Mass customization can also be structured around added customer convenience. For example, even a mass-produced, standardized item may be hard to find. Customization can be structured around saving the user the time he might otherwise spend finding it and buying it, which adds to the overall transaction cost. Remember our investment banker – time is money. Imagine you are producing customized suits. The customer selects the fabric and the cut of the suit, and then supplies his measurements. That particular suit might also be available mass produced at a department store. But the customer does not have to go there and try on suits, still no guarantee that he will find the right one.

Time is money

In the case of a customized newspaper it means that you will get only the information that you pre-selected according to your interests. The newspaper you get today might give you the same information as a customized one but that might be buried under heaps of other stuff that you do not really care about. Your customized paper will only give you the stock prices for the ten stocks that you own so you do not have to go through columns of minute numbers.

Status and entertainment

While much of the rationale for eCommerce is built around eminently practical considerations – most prominently, price and convenience – psychological elements are also important, as indeed they always have been in retailing.

Most people enjoy having things that others admire, whether it be good art, well-cut clothes, good wine or a fancy car – the more distinctive the better. But while the greatest status attaches to rare items – say Old Master paintings or vintage Ferraris – new products, even mass-produced ones, can become status symbols through customization. The trick is to customize only some features of the product and leave the rest of the production process untouched. It is a bit like developing a photograph.

New products can become status symbols through customization

The production process for developing the pictures is highly standardized and automated, but an artist can turn an ordinary negative into something special.

A consumer can also have fun by putting her own stamp on a standardized product by designing the terms of customization. You might find that quite a few people will design and order their customized product just for the sake of designing it themselves. This can be a watch with a face they choose themselves or a pair of skis with their name on them. Of course, there are also combinations, for example custom-made bikes, that are probably ordered mainly to suit the customer's exact measurements, but with additional design features such as a special paint job and the customer's name.

With fun as a buying criterion we are coming back to the distinction between the fun Internet surfer and the convenience surfer. Most likely the fun surfer will be the one who is fascinated by the online design possibilities and finds playing around with them enjoyable in itself. Nevertheless, the functionality should be designed also for the convenience surfer who might enjoy the web site's possibilities but does not want to play around with it for ages. He would rather get finished quickly and still obtain superior results.

Price

Still, for all the value-added customization potential in our new global e-village, some customers are motivated primarily by price, and would be perfectly content to buy a standard item if it is also the least expensive alternative. However, because of the inherent economies of Internet retailing, it often becomes possible to customize and still be the lowest cost choice. When you take out the cost of standing inventory, distribution, store rental and the risk of not selling something, the expense of custom design and assembly is not all that forbidding. We now examine what effect customization can have on the cost position of the manufacturer.

> **Because of the inherent economies of Internet retailing, it often becomes possible to customize and still be the lowest cost choice**

There are additional savings. Apart from actually being less expensive upon delivery, the product can also save the customer after delivery because there is no need for additional alterations. It would be cheaper to buy a customized $220 suit that is delivered in a week than a $190 suit if you need to spend $50 to shorten the sleeves of the jacket and widen the waistband, and, on top of that, wait two weeks to take delivery.

The customer can also enjoy price advantages if he can select the product features he wants, to be assembled from scratch, without extraneous features that are included in the standard product but that really have no value for him. And the cost for custom alterations of standard products can be considerable, as anyone who has ever tried to customize a standard software product such as SAP will readily admit.

The customer, therefore, has to take into account total cost, and it is in the retailer's interest to build this thinking into his sales pitch. Take the example of a company that prints business cards for corporate accounts. The printer's usual procedure is to execute orders almost unthinkingly. The design is standard and the exact text for the cards is supplied by a designated employee of the customer. That person has to make sure that the name is spelled correctly, the cards are reordered ahead of time so no one will run out, and they all adhere to the corporate identity standards. Every time a new employee is hired, or someone is promoted, or the organization structure is changed (and with it job titles) new name cards have to be printed. The value added in that job is basically zero, but it is nevertheless quite a lot of work (especially since more and more companies tend to restructure themselves ever other year or to merge with other companies).

Imagine that all employees could order their business cards over an Intranet or Internet application directly from their desk

Now imagine that all employees could order their business cards over an Intranet or Internet application directly from their desk. The company would establish once what the basic criteria for all their business cards are, such as the size of the card, the type of paper and the basic layout, including the company logo and the type set. People could order their cards themselves when they run out or their information has changed, and can even have them delivered wherever they happen to be working, instead of being routed to their home office. People can have their current mobile phone number and home fax number on the cards if they wish, or they can choose not to. So apart from making the whole thing easier the new process also allows every employee to customize their cards within the limits of the corporate identity.

At the same time it is also an easy and efficient way to ensure that business cards for employees in different countries meet predefined standards, because the business cards for all employees all over the world can now be printed in one central location without the inconveniences, time delays and inflexibility that are usually associated with a centralized process.

A function within the company – namely that of coordinating the business card ordering process – is made superfluous, which saves the company money and at the same time allows for higher flexibility through direct communication between the end customer and the manufacturer. The function of coordinating business card orders not only costs money, but also creates an unnecessary bottleneck in the whole process. So even if the cards should cost a little more ordered online by individuals it would still pay off for the company because the new process allows them to save money on staff. In this example, however, there is no reason why the cards would cost more; if the employee types in all the information himself and the information is transferred directly to a digital printing press, customized cards should actually cost less, because it also helps to save money in the production process. Therefore, lower price as a buying criterion can also mean that even if the price for the product itself is actually the same or even slightly higher, the whole process can save the customer's internal cost.

So possible reasons for buying customized products are customization itself, added convenience, status and fun and lower overall price. Appreciating which of these features are a selling point for targeted customers requires the ability to look at customization from the viewpoint of customers first, because this is where every new strategy, product development or business idea should start. If there is no value added for the customer you do not have a business case. There is no value proposition and no reason for the customer to buy your product. Once you have found a value added for the customer you have to take a step back and look at what it means aggregated over all customers and the consequences for your business.

> **Once you have found a value added for the customer you have to take a step back and look at what it means aggregated over all customers and the consequences for your business**

We now come to what those customer needs mean for the manufacturer on an aggregated level. What is the competitive advantage of customization for the manufacturer and what results does he anticipate on the revenue and the cost sides? On the revenue side customized production can address a larger market, help to achieve a higher market share by addressing more customer needs or foster customer loyalty. On the cost side customized production can reduce costs through better planning options, real-time market research and cutting production costs directly by outsourcing part of the process to the customer. We now look at each of those points in more detail.

Increased revenue through customization

If you want to increase your total revenue you can increase either the number of products you sell or the price of those products. Let us have a look at the number of products first.

In mass production products were produced for the average needs and tastes of the average user. But this will yield satisfactory results only if the actual desires of the customers are very similar. If you produce a stereo system only in black and this happens to be the preferred colour of 90 per cent of the potential customers anyway you have not satisfied only 10 per cent of potential customers. If you decide to produce suits in only ten different sizes you might find that you are not fulfilling the needs of about 70 per cent of your potential customer base. After all tastes are one thing – and in stereos they are secondary to the quality of the sound the thing makes – but variations in shape and body type cannot be denied.

Therefore, the distribution of needs and tastes also determines the size of the additional customer potential that can be tapped through customization. Customization of suits in the example would open up a market of 70 per cent of suit buyers whereas a variation of colour in stereo systems would only yield an additional customer base of 10 per cent. Not that the people who do not get suits that fit them will go naked. Instead they will buy suits that do not fit them.

So the total market for suits will probably not increase through customization, but the people who had to buy ill-fitting suits so far will shift their buying power from their previous manufacturer to you. You increase your share of a stable total market by adapting your product to the needs of customers who have so far remained unsatisfied.

You increase your share of a stable total market by adapting your product to the needs of customers who have so far remained unsatisfied

Customization can also be the basis to increase the total market, of course, when latent desires are aroused by the appearance of new options. This is especially the case when the fun of designing the product and the cachet of owning a customized product are key criteria for buying. An example for this would be Swatch. Through their variations and hundreds of different models they have actually increased the market for watches because people might now own several watches, whereas previously they only owned one.

Apart from increasing revenue by increasing the total market or increasing your share in a given market you can also increase prices. This will not work, of course, if the prime reason for the customer to buy your customized products is a lower price. If the reasons are a better fit, added convenience, or fun and status, there is actually a higher customer benefit which can also justify a higher price. In fact, if you are still selling standardized products in parallel to your customized products it might be advisable to sell them for slightly higher prices if you do not want to endanger your standard product line.

Customization might also pay off over the course of time by engendering higher customer loyalty. If your customer has been satisfied by the customized product because it was exactly what he was looking for there is a good chance that next time he needs the same product he will buy it from you again. This is true for any product, of course, but for customized products there is an additional reason for customers to return to the manufacturer of the first product: since you still have all the customization data on file, the customer does not have to go through the whole process of customization again.

This is especially valuable if the customer just wants to change some features while keeping others the same. If the customer has bought a customized shirt and now wants to buy another one but in a different colour, all the data about the size and the cut of the shirt remain the same and will be readily provided by the web site. This fact shows the importance of getting the customer the first time he buys a customized product because once all the customization information is available on a competitor's web site it becomes difficult to get the customer back.

To get the correct measures for a first-time customer therefore – especially for clothes and shoes – is a process where it makes sense for the manufacturer to spend more money, because it is actually an investment in the future relationship with the customer. Some customers might be reluctant to take their measurements themselves even if a step-by-step guide on the screen explains exactly what to do. When asked to take their chest measurement people might feel insecure because they do not know if they should breathe in or out, at what exact height they should measure, and how tight they should pull the tape measure. They might feel that they need the assistance of a qualified tailor.

Once all the customization information is available on a competitor's web site it becomes difficult to get the customer back

This could actually be the basis for a new 'retailor' business. A 'retailor' with a web presence would have small outlets in high-traffic locations and customers who want to buy custom-made clothes could go to the 'retailor' and get their measurements. The 'retailor' would take the measurement like a regular tailor, but instead of producing the clothes himself he would serve as a qualified data entry point for customization manufacturers. The 'retailor' would enter the measures into the customization web site of participating clothes manufacturers and get paid a commission by the manufacturer for any first-time customer. After that, the manufacturer would own the customer. Because customization web sites offer more incentives for higher customer loyalty than retailers selling standardized products the investment in any first-time customer can quickly pay off.

Reduced costs through customization

If your unique selling proposition is lower prices, then you have to sell the mass-customized products below the current prices for standardized products. Since the margins today for most products are already very slim, this necessarily means that you have to reduce costs. But even if your selling proposition is added convenience or a product that exactly fits the customer's needs, cost reduction possibilities might still be very interesting, even if you do not reduce your prices immediately. Bear in mind, however, that a price umbrella usually does not last for long on the Internet and will attract competition.

One of the most important advantages of mass customization is the fact that you do not have to stock an inventory of finished products any more. This means there is no capital tied up in warehouses and there is no risk of being left with unwanted stock. This can offer considerable cost advantages, especially in industries where customer tastes shift quickly and the danger of unsellable overstocks is relatively high.

> **Bear in mind that a price umbrella usually does not last for long on the internet and will attract competition**

Take the fashion industry as an example. Clothing companies do not really know what customers will want season after season, but they must produce and ship their designs anyway. For some items this might mean that large quantities are produced and never sold at retail. Even for items that do sell very well there is a considerable stock risk because it is very difficult to predict when the demand will drop. If the producer has anticipated that the sales will stay on the same level for another two weeks and they suddenly drop instead, he is stuck with two weeks' stock in his warehouse that no one wants. In the fashion industry about 50 per cent of all garments are sold below the regular price in order to clear stock.

So if you can mass customize your fashion products and sell them at the regular price you are already enjoying a considerable advantage. Since the mass customizer only produces based on customer orders there is no risk of not selling the product or not selling it for the full price. If 50 per cent of standardized products have to be sold with a 50 per cent discount – not an unrealistic figure – the mass customizer already enjoys an advantage of 25 per cent although the prices for the consumer have not changed.

> **In the fashion industry about 50 per cent of all garments are sold below the regular price in order to clear stocks**

And the situation for the manufacturers of standardized products is not going to get better. Changes in fashion come faster and faster, and since the consumers have learned by now that a large percentage of clothes will go on sale relatively quickly, they actually wait for sales even when they find something they like. This change in consumer behaviour will lead to an even higher percentage of clothes that cannot be sold for the full price.

In the CD business, where predicting consumer behaviour is also very difficult, on average about 15 per cent of CDs go unsold, but for some titles this rate can be as high as 70 or 80 per cent. In contrast to the fashion industry, however, the CD industry usually prefers to shred the surplus CDs instead of selling them for reduced rates to avoid having consumers waiting for reduced prices.

The examples show that there is considerable cost-saving potential involved because the mass customizer does not have to produce large stocks of merchandise. The advantages are biggest in the industries where the prediction of customer behaviour is most difficult and the demand can change quickly. Since companies in all industries suffer today from an increasing uncertainty in planning and predicting the market, this shows that there might be quite considerable potential for mass customization.

Of course, the mass customizer also has to predict and plan customer behaviour but on a different level. Dell Computers, which produces every PC to the order of a customer, does not have to predict any more how many computers with specific processors, motherboard and memory built into one particular PC they will sell because the different modules are put together only after orders have been received. Nevertheless, Dell still has to predict how many of the different modules they will sell in total, because manufacturers of CD-ROMs, monitors and processors have lead times of several weeks or even months, compared to Dell's assembly and delivery within a few days. But the complexity of predicting customer demand is greatly reduced. Dell only has to predict how many of a certain CD-ROM it will sell in total in all its computers, which is difficult enough, but not in what combination with what other modules. It orders components in general but manufactures and ships in particular, whereas other companies must order, manufacture and ship in particular, which in aggregate is a much more complex and error-prone scenario.

Connections to customers, suppliers, and others who might become advocates of the web site product become important

At the same time, the manufacturer also gets very valuable information through the orders of individual customers. Dell will know a lot sooner if consumer demand for a specific product changes than will its competitors who produce standardized products that are sold through regular retail channels. This information can be used to design products and offer customization options long before the competition even notices that the demand has changed. We will look at this in more detail in a later chapter.

In order to reap the full cost benefit of the Internet, all processes, systems and work flow have to be integrated or it is not going to work. Connections to customers, suppliers, and others who might become advocates of the web site product, as in Amazon's affiliate programme, become important. Integration of information generated within the company is just as important. Only streamlined processes with seamless flows of information make mass customization, customized service and online auctions economically feasible.

Integration of the Internet interface with the internal order entry system saves considerable amounts of money because the customer does the work of typing in the order and verifying that her order is recorded correctly. This not only eliminates the need for an order entry department for Internet sales, it also greatly reduces the need for a customer service department. Customer service centres are usually busy answering customer inquiries about the status of delivery or complaints about the wrong product that has been delivered.

Customer entry of orders cuts down on the volume of complaints about wrong orders. Since the customer can check the status of the order himself on the Internet there is no need to ring the call centre. So you are actually outsourcing your order entry and customer service to the customer. The beauty of it is that the transfer of tasks to the customer reduces cost and is at the same time viewed by the customer as added convenience.

The customer does the work

In this sense, the Internet can be compared to automatic teller machines (ATMs), which help banks save considerable costs and also offer added convenience for the customer. The customer has the advantage of being able to draw money on a round-the-clock basis and can even get service in his own language when travelling abroad. And the self-service at the ATM is a lot quicker than going to a teller. Many of us have probably not transacted through a teller in years.

However, online order entry is just a first step. The Internet is not just another sales channel that can be added to the existing organization without changing anything else. If you want to offer customized products you must generate an integrated information flow from the customer to order entry, accounts receivable, production, warehouses, and even suppliers and transport companies. This is the only way to ensure that the customer will get accurate information about production and delivery status. While integrating all processes in one or several systems is necessary to offer customized products with all the value-added services it also helps to ensure considerable internal operating savings.

So do not be fooled into thinking that it is enough to design a superior web site. First of all you will not be able to offer the functionality that customers expect without integrating your internal processes and adapting them to the new medium, and second you will not be able to get the full benefit of transaction cost reduction if it is business as usual inside the company. If there is a possibility to cut costs you had better take advantage of it because someone else surely will. Today's excessive overhead is tomorrow's e-business proposition for someone else. On the Internet it will not be long before your customers know who has the best value for money.

Reduced process and internal costs do not mean that the total product cost will come down. Depending on the product and the additional steps in the production cycle that have to be implemented in order to customize, the production costs can actually be higher. But customers' willingness to pay might also go up because the customized product offers special features and added convenience. It is difficult to say whether the prices will go up or down because it depends on the individual market, the production process and the extent of customization options.

Today's excessive overhead is tomorrow's e-business proposition for someone else

The Internet will lead to greater transparency in the market, however, which will usually result in fiercer competition and shrinking margins. But since customization upsets the basic assumption that products are more or less interchangeable, as they are in mass-production markets, firms can develop a loyal following for their customized products, thereby justifying higher prices in their customers' minds.

On the Internet it will not be long before your customers know who has the best value for money

One of the main advantages of mass customization is that you have less need to compete on price, unless price is your unique selling proposition. Since the products are differentiated from the standardized mass-produced products, you have created a quasi-monopoly that allows you to charge higher prices which will last until your competitors also start to customize their products. So the first mover advantage is crucial again. However, as the first-mover you will also have the advantage of real-time market research, which, as we will see, can help you stay ahead of the second-mover competition after you have accumulated a larger customer base. If a company constantly invents new product and customization possibilities it might be able to keep the monopoly advantage and thus does not have to compete on price.

Chapter 15

Online product configuration

The single most important web site feature for selling customized products is a customer interface that helps the customer to find or define what he actually wants. This poses two challenges: the first is effectively to communicate the different options that are available, and can be chosen online. We have already discussed the different possibilities for communicating product features via the web. Once you have effectively communicated the options, the second challenge

The single most important web site feature for selling customized products is a customer interface that helps the customer to find or define what he actually wants

is to help the customer define and locate the product that he actually wants. That is what this chapter is about.

The challenge

The challenge is designing the individualization process using the web site as the customer interface and the tool for customization. As with customized communication, this process of individualizing products and services can either be initiated by the buyer (active customization) or by the seller (passive customization).

For active customization the key to success is a web site design that makes it convenient to input all the information necessary to customize the customer's product. The customer has to be able to determine the product configuration without being overwhelmed by the entire selection of possible options and features. Some choices can be almost infinitely variable, such as the length of the sleeves of a shirt. Others would only offer a discreet number of options, for instance the different types of processors that can be built into a PC.

For every choice there should always be a default option, which represents your recommendation if the customer cannot make up his mind about, say, the ten different buttons for your customized shirt. Those default options can also be interactive. If your customer has already selected a blue business shirt you would automatically prompt blue buttons as the default option. For a white shirt you would prompt white buttons. The customer always has the choice to order a white shirt with pink buttons, of course, by clicking on a different option.

However, for some products, making the choices on the web site is harder. Depending on the product you offer you could make a virtual sales assistant available to help the customer come up with a unique product that satisfies his needs. It is especially important to help the customer if the design is an important part of the customization and the look of the product. Imagine you give your customers the opportunity to design their own business cards. Some people love designing things and are really good at it. Others have their talents, but design and layout are not among them. So if you do not support them in coming up with a good design, they are not going to buy the cards because they do not like the look of them. Even worse they might actually buy the cards and show them to other people who as a result will never turn up on your site.

As with customized communication, you can have a design assistant available for beginners. The designer would ask the customer a few questions, such as whether the card is for personal or business use or if she wants a more conservative or innovative design. The customer would have to enter the personal details she wants printed on the card first because one design might look good with a short name and just the address but look horrible with a long name, job title, home and work addresses, fax number, mobile number, two email addresses and a company logo.

The design assistant would take these factors into consideration and then come up with, say, five different proposals of nicely designed cards for the customer to choose from. Depending on how complicated the product you are selling is and how well designed your virtual sales assistant is, you could also offer the option of talking to a human sales representative either through email or through a direct call-back functionality.

For the expert or hobby designer, the web site would still offer all options that you would usually expect when you are a designer: several thousand different fonts, infinite selection of colours, and the possibility to import pictures or graphics, to name a few. Offer these choices to the beginner and he may never buy a business card from you.

You must update and reprogram your virtual sales assistant regularly to ensure that the choices are up to date

The design assistant that has just been described relies on information that has been entered by the company that runs the web site. This ensures that it can influence the choices and options and maintain a high standard of quality. It also means that you must update and reprogram your virtual sales assistant regularly to ensure that the choices are up to date. If your customer asks you for a home computer for under $1,000 that she can use for Internet access and easy word-processing activities, the optimal recommendation that the virtual sales assistant would make today might be quite different from the recommendation six months from now.

But the virtual sales assistant does not necessarily have to be updated regularly by the owner of the web site. It could also update itself based on user preferences and ongoing market information. Customized CDs are a good example: the customer has to be guided through the customization process without getting the impression of having to choose between millions of available titles. To narrow down the number of choices, the customer needs to have the opportunity to provide personal input on a number of parameters, such as the music type, the name of the band, the publishing year, the occasion for which the CD is being bought and many others.

There are tools available that support this process and increase customer convenience. After a series of transactions, the company can gather enough knowledge about customer preferences so it can more precisely pre-select titles to feature on its home page for individual customers, and thus make the process simpler.

If somebody has put eight soul music CDs in his shopping cart, his taste is pretty clear. These data set the stage for passive customization. It is possible to offer a ninth soul CD to the customer during the session. Because this CD is likely to fit his taste, but he did not know about it before, it might be perceived as a value-adding service offering and will enhance customer loyalty.

The criteria

The criteria that can be used to suggest titles to one customer can be based on the tastes and selections of other customers. Virtual bookstores can suggest new books to customers based on the buying patterns of other customers. Virtual sales assistants that draw their intelligence out of the choices of others are a very useful option for items like books or CDs, where the possible choices number in the millions and subjective criteria are so important. They also have the advantage for the retailer of being constantly updated without additional cost because they use information entered by the customer. This type of virtual sales assistant only works, however, if the number of customers on your site has reached a certain critical mass, whereas the design assistant, as in the business card example mentioned before, is based on criteria that are entered by the retailer himself from the outset.

User-generated content can serve not only as the basis for virtual sales assistants but directly as a value-added feature

User-generated content can serve not only as the basis for virtual sales assistants but directly as a value-added feature. When the user customizes a product for himself on the web site, he might at the same time create product specifications or designs that are actually valuable for other customers. If the user agrees, those designs can also be made available for other users and further enhance the attractiveness of the web site.

Take the example of a site that sells custom-made carpets. The user can choose between different carpet sizes, colours, shapes and the quality of the material. The carpet is then woven or knotted according to the customer's specifications. Most people will find it easy to determine the size and the shape of the carpet according to the room in which they want to put it. Selecting the quality of the material and the production type – weaving or knotting, number of knots, and so on – is usually not too difficult because it will be largely determined by whether it is a wall carpet or a floor carpet, by the price for the different production types and materials and by the depth of the customer's pockets.

Selecting the colours, however, might give some people a headache. The problem is not choosing the colours on the screen, because you can always offer the option of mailing real fabric samples to the customer. The challenge for most customers is to come up with a carpet design that they really like. The number of choices is infinite and could be anything from a solid-coloured blue to a modern Dali painting or a drawing by the customer's little daughter. Not all designs will look good when produced as carpets. And not every buyer of a carpet is a gifted designer. But some of your customers are, so why not make the designs of these customers available to everyone?

Every time a customer designs a carpet for himself you could ask him if he wants to make the design available to other users. He would then have to answer a few questions about the design, such as whether it is modern or classic, abstract, concrete, copied from another medium, and so forth. The web site could add such features as the predominant colour that is used in the design. When a customer is looking for a modern abstract design with predominantly turquoise and blue colours, the web site would list all designs that fulfil these criteria ranked in the order of previously selected designs.

These and other digitized characteristics of the design will make it easier for other customers to find their preferred design once the web site has accumulated a substantial database of designs. This database of user-generated content can serve as a reservoir of ideas for customers so they get some impetus and encouragement for designing their own carpet. It can also serve as a catalogue of possible carpet designs that customers can simply select. The data can also be organized around certain general criteria for customers who have no firm ideas of their own.

If a carpet design of one customer is selected for production by another it could lead to revenue for the designer. The web site could offer to pay a small percentage of every carpet sale that uses one particular design to the original designer. The original designer would get a cheque or have the money transferred directly to her account on a monthly basis, based on the revenue that has been generated. This incentive would probably very quickly also have another effect. It could attract a large number of hobby, student or professional designers who would create designs on your site without ever planning to buy a carpet.

But the site could also function as a showcase for their work, and thus gain considerable reputation for the trader. Designers could specify prices for which they want to sell their designs, which would have to be paid by the customer on top of the production of the carpet itself. They might also choose to offer limited editions of their designs. The designs could even be auctioned and for a very successful design the price might rise considerably once the limited edition comes to an end. For the carpet manufacturer this might generate a totally new market where the carpets become designer objects.

In order to gain publicity the web site might even want to produce limited editions with well-known designers like Hundertwasser and then run a marketing campaign around the Hundertwasser limited edition. Arrangements with art galleries might be another interesting option.

There could, too, also be arrangements with celebrities who also happen to draw. The web site could publish carpet design bestseller lists. Or the site could select a design per month for a bargain price.

In the beginning when the design database is still rather small and not very attractive for the user, the web site could run design contests in conjunction with design schools. The best design would be awarded a cash prize but all designs that enter the competition agree to be made available on the web site later, with remuneration to the artist for carpets sold.

Depending on what type of carpets and what type of customers the web site wants to focus on, the manufacturer would not even have to develop a new production technique. For hand-knotted carpets there is no difference in the cost or production technology no matter what design the customer chooses. It is actually possible today to have a carpet knotted according to your design; it is just that very few people even know about this option. For machine-woven carpets, changes in production technology might be necessary in order to accommodate the change of design from one carpet to the next.

A clearly arranged, self-learning selection process and a virtual sales assistant can help the novice customer quickly select the product he wants

The carpet example shows that through the new customization options an array of possibilities open up. A similar approach could be used for any product where design is an important buying criterion, but where production has the benefits of scale. This could go from self-designed bed sheets to floor tiles and wallpaper. The customization is not necessarily done by the customer himself, but by other customers or designers who create the design. The actual customer then only has to select the design he likes out of the possibilities, if he does not want to do it himself.

So far we have discussed the different web site functions that help a new customer to select what he wants. A clearly arranged, self-learning selection process and a virtual sales assistant can help the novice customer quickly select the product he wants. But a well-managed web site will have not only first-time customers.

If the first-time customer has been satisfied with the buying experience and the value for money, he will become a loyal customer. In that case you can very much facilitate the customization process. Since you already know what he bought last time, you can start to customize the user interface as soon as the customer logs on. This is also another incentive for the customer to identify himself with the web site at the beginning of the process.

The choices

The number of choices you can offer to customize your product is limited only by the production possibilities and the quality of the virtual sales assistant. The trick is to offer thousands of choices disguised as an intimate personal retail relationship. The total number of choices is not the problem, because the customer does not have to see them all at the same time. It is very important, however, that the customer can see a running count for price changes every time he adds an option. If you only display the price at the very end of the selection process, the customer will most likely go back several times, change individual features and see how it affects the total price. The underlying pricing structure and discounts for various combinations of modules can be quite complex. The advantage on the Internet is that the customer does not have to understand the underlying logic if you display the current price for the selected item at any time. He can just choose the option and see how it affects the price. (We discuss possibilities of customizing pricing later.)

The number of choices you can offer to customize your product is limited only by the production possibilities and the quality of the virtual sales assistant

The same is also true for delivery time. If you only display the delivery time at the end of the specification process for a computer, the customer might have configured the whole computer only to find out that he has to wait two months until it is shipped. He does not know, however, why this is so, and he probably does not care, but the longer he has to wait the more annoyed he will be. If the delivery time is continuously displayed while he is selecting the different modules for a PC, he will notice that the delivery time is always one week and suddenly jumps to two months upon selection of a specific monitor. This can be the case if the particular monitor is out of stock and will not be delivered before the two months' period. When the customer immediately sees that the choice of this particular monitor will make the delivery time jump from a week to two months, he might decide to choose a different monitor. If the delivery time is only displayed at the end of the process the customer might be dissatisfied with the fact that he has to wait two months, have little patience to find out why, and go looking for another web site to get what he wants. Again, offering this functionality requires having an integrated IT system that links the customer interface with the warehouse and ideally even the supplier's IT systems.

After the selection process is finished and the customer has found or configured the product he desires, the web site should display the results of the selection process. For a customized computer this would mean displaying all the components that the customer has selected. For a customized CD it would mean displaying the summary of titles that the customer has chosen.

If there is any chance of visualizing the product, this is the time to do it. For a customized bike the web site would display a picture of the whole bike together with all the features the customer has selected and with the colouring he has chosen.

Once the customer has confirmed that this is actually the item he wants, the next step is to obtain the necessary personal customer data: name, email address, delivery address, form of payment. If the customer is a repeat customer, all the information would already be entered from the previous purchase and the customer would be offered the chance to change any details that might not be correct any more – the customer might want to charge to a different credit card this time or have the product delivered to a different address. For added convenience some web sites offer a one-click buying option that uses all the information from the last purchase.

For added convenience some web sites offer a one-click buying option that uses all the information from the last purchase

If you are planning to use customer passwords to identify the customer the next time around, it is also a good idea to let the customer choose his log-in name and password now. Unless you are dealing with high-security transactions it is a good idea to let the customer choose his own password because that is the best way he will actually remember the password the next time around. If you happily inform him that his new password is WH4J86BM the chances that he will readily identify himself with that password on the next log-in are rather slim. And in the event the user forgets the self-chosen password, it has become common practice to ask the user for a critical question and answer at the time of the first log-in, which can be used for verification. So at the first log-in the user would choose, for example, 'What was the name of my first dog?' as a question and also enter the answer to that question. If he ever forgets his password the web site will ask him for the name of his first dog in order to identify her.

Once the customer has entered or confirmed the personal details the order can be completed. The web site can now immediately send an email that confirms the order, price, and delivery time. The next email could confirm that the product has actually been shipped and when it will arrive. In those cases, the primary objective of the mailings is to give the customer peace of mind. Of course, as outlined in the chapter about customized communication, the customer should have the choice not to receive those mailings. The customer should also immediately be notified by email if there is any change to the agreed delivery time. Proactive customer information is a way to ensure customer trust and loyalty, but it can also save you considerable costs in your call centre. Apart from informing the customer via email, the web site should offer the option of active order tracking by the customer.

Chapter 16

Production of customized products

Advantages and disadvantages

Internet sites enjoy scale advantages because they usually get better as their customer base grows. When you have a bricks and mortar store it can only grow to a certain size. Growing any further would not make sense, because there may not be enough potential customers who live in the area to make it worthwhile. For the retailer it makes more sense to offer a second store in a different location

Internet sites enjoy scale advantages because they usually get better as their customer base grows

and to replicate the existing successful formula instead of continually expanding that one store. So when bricks and mortar businesses grow bigger they have more outlets but the service level and selection in the individual outlet do not necessarily increase.

On the Internet the situation is quite different. There are no theoretical limits to the number of articles that an Internet store can carry just as there are no limits to the potential customer base, although building a distribution system presents problems of its own. The bigger the store, however, the bigger the possible advantages for the customer. A business with a larger customer base can offer more user-generated content and more different options for customization. Imagine that for manufacturing reasons you can only produce a product in a certain colour in a given production cycle – say a week – if you have at least 100 customers who want that colour. If you only sell 1,000 products a week you can produce a maximum of 10 different colours, assuming demand is distributed evenly between the colours. Probably you will be able to produce fewer, because customer desires will most likely be split unevenly between the different colours. If you are selling one million products a week, however, you can offer the customer a maximum of 10,000 different colours.

> There are no theoretical limits to the number of articles that an Internet store can carry

While it probably does not make sense to offer that many colours from a customer perspective, because the choice would only be confusing, it serves to outline the underlying principle. The more customers you have the more choices you can offer and still produce efficiently.

The Internet, therefore, has an inherent tendency to favour the development of very large, market-dominating companies because there is no incentive to buy from companies that offer a limited selection when a company that offers ten times as many choices is only one mouse click away. This underscores again the importance of the first-mover advantage. If someone else has already built a large customer base when you enter the market, that company can already offer many customization options that you cannot because you just do not have the market for it yet. An additional danger is that the competitor does not necessarily have to be one of your traditional competitors. A competitor who starts to build his customer base in a different country or even with a different product might go unnoticed until he has reached a considerable size and then just rolls out his capabilities to other countries and products.

> The Internet has an inherent tendency to favour the development of very large, market-dominating companies

Customized production relies primarily on the customer to design the product. The options that are available have to be predefined by the producer, however, otherwise customers are going to specify features that are economically or technically impossible to produce. The company needs to sell products that lend themselves to mass customization through processes that combine economies of scale with flexibility, unit by unit.

Modularization

In many cases, the key to cost-effective mass customization will be products built from various modules that can be personalized and combined. Think of LEGO toys: there are a few basic pieces in different shapes and colours that all fit together. These basics are sufficient for children to build almost anything they can imagine. Likewise, when you order a Dell computer, for each of the modules – processor, hard drive, monitor, disk drives, CD-ROM, and so on – you select from a range of choices and therefore create the machine that fits your needs.

Modularization increases the external variety of choices available to the customer while at the same time keeping the internal variety of parts and production processes at manageable levels. Those modules with a long production lead time should have the greatest measure of standardization, whereas elements that can be changed quickly during the production process can be offered in more variations.

Even products that are not manufactured from modules can offer mass customization potential

But even products that are not manufactured from modules can offer mass customization potential, as long as the customization is limited to a few steps in the production process. Internal variety can also be reduced if the production process uses identical materials. Variety only emerges at the end of the process. The aim is to keep costs down but at the same time offer variations that mean the most to the customer.

The fashion industry offers an excellent example of mass customization that provides high external variety while at the same time keeping the internal variety to a minimum. The production process for a customized pair of jeans differs from that for standard jeans by only two steps. The customized jeans can use the same fabric, the same sewing machines, the same production facilities and the same washing machines. They actually differ because they are cut to the customer's size individually, while standard jeans are cut many at a time, and they are delivered to the customer individually while standard jeans are delivered in bulk to the store.

Some features can only be customized in discrete steps while others can also offer continuous customization options. Jeans, for example, could be produced in any length the customer wants. From the production process there is no need to offer only one-inch increments for the length of the jeans. Hard-disk drives for PCs theoretically could also be produced with any capacity the customer might want. It is much more economical to offer them only in a few different sizes, especially since they have quite a long development and production lead time.

> **The production process for a customized pair of jeans differs from that for standard jeans by only two steps**

Whether a product is 'customizable' depends very much on its design. When Dell started to build computers to order, computers were already built out of modules, so there was no need to redesign the product. For other products that might not be the case. To be able to produce and sell a mass-customized product effectively, you might have to redesign the product first. If there is a cost increase through the customization you have to ensure that the increase will be covered by a price premium that the customer is willing to pay.

A modular product redesign might also have other advantages for the customer. The customer might want to change something after he has bought it if his need or taste changes. This would give the manufacturer the opportunity to start a lucrative spare parts business on his web site. Selling spare parts or exchange modules keeps you in touch with customers and offers numerous cross-selling opportunities.

When you are producing customized products, selling spare parts or exchange modules might not be as easy as it looks because the original product might be unique if it was customized. So when you offer spare parts on your web site you also have to make sure that the customer can actually find the exact spare part that he needs. If you are selling a computer that is built to order and your customer contacts you 12 months later to try to buy an extension to his existing system or a replacement of the CD-ROM, you had better know exactly how his original system was configured because otherwise you might mail him a part that will not work with the rest of the existing system.

One bright note is that your competitors will have the same problem. Since a competitor will not have the customization information that you have it will be almost impossible for them to sell the correct part. Therefore, the spare part and extension business can be very lucrative because it is basically a monopoly situation. Of course, the manufacturer should refrain from acting too much like a monopolist if he is also interested in loyal customers.

In many cases personal customization will be impossible because the features that lend themselves to customization are truly custom, and cannot be built on any economically viable scale. In car production, for example, it would be extremely costly to let every customer choose the colour and complete design of his car individually out of all colours that can be designed on the web (several million) because the costs of changing colour and design from one car to the next in the production process could be quite high. So the old rule of Henry Ford that 'The customer can have the car in any color he wants, as long as it's black' could change to 'The customer can have the car in any color he wants, as long as there are at least 99 other people in the world who want the same color this month.'

The web offers unique opportunities to aggregate individuals all over the world to find a group large enough to make a certain production economically possible. The car maker could, for example, design a special feature car that is offered on the Internet for a limited period of time and will only be produced at all if a predetermined number of people sign up for it.

Whereas most of the production options we have discussed so far have been actively customized by the customer, passive customization by the manufacturer also plays an important role.

When the production process allows, a manufacturer can suggest a few combinations of product features each month that will be produced if enough customers want it. As the manufacturer develops experience with this option over time, he will be able to estimate the number of customers who will choose a certain product feature if offered for a certain price. Therefore it will no longer be necessary to tell the customer that the production will depend on the number of other customers who select the same feature. The manufacturer can bear the risk because he knows from experience how many people will select a certain feature within a certain period.

The old rule of Henry Ford that 'The customer can have the car in any color he wants, as long as it's black' could change to 'The customer can have the car in any color he wants, as long as there are at least 99 other people in the world who want the same color this month'

The number of people who must choose a certain feature before it gets produced can also vary. It depends on the costs of the production process but also on the price the individual customer is willing to pay. (We discuss the topic of customized pricing later.)

Selling directly to your customer also changes other things that people in your industry might think are fundamental to their business. For example, your product packaging no longer has to be designed for advertising and shelf space. Instead what the product will look like when it is delivered becomes more important. Similar changes are true for the location of your company: it is no longer important to be close to where your customers live. Instead you might find that it is critical to be close to the Federal Express or UPS hub to ensure that all orders you receive on one particular day will go out overnight.

In order to reap the full benefits of customized products, all relevant processes within the company have to be integrated into one networked IT system. The order from the customer ideally should go directly into the production system, warehousing systems, supplier systems and accounts receivable. As long as there are system breaks the company has to bear higher cost of varying its production process and is not reaping the full benefit of eCommerce. If every variation the customer chooses has to be individually handled by an employee who has to check availability of the necessary parts, production capacity, and so on, the whole process will be so costly that customization will become uneconomical compared to standardized products.

Database needs

When you only customize communication as already outlined in previous chapters you might get away with a database that only involves the customer interface and previous buying patterns. If we are talking about customized production, however, you need a database that involves the whole production cycle, work flow management back to the warehouse content or just in time delivery by suppliers. Those companies that use customization as a catalyst for the whole business process redesign are likely to reap the greatest benefit. They can offer functionality for their customers that remains wishful thinking for their competitors and they can use the process integration for further cost saving.

Those companies that use customization as a catalyst for the whole business process redesign are likely to reap the greatest benefit

When we are talking about process redesign throughout the whole organization, we are talking big budgets. You need board-level support to start a process redesign like that and it has to involve the whole company. It is impossible to delegate it to any single department. With the necessary integration needs, no single department could effectively house the whole thing, not strategy, marketing, R&D, or information technology. All are involved.

It might be better to build the new business model and then migrate the rest of the organization on to it. You can perform all the functions in-house, or outsource some or all of them. Seamless integration is the key element. Whether you perform all functions yourself or none of them makes no difference as long as all the process steps are properly integrated. Your value addition that is hardest to copy would be the process integration of all those functions that results in a customized customer experience.

Besides a successful web interface the biggest challenge is to integrate the back office and actually be able to fulfil the customer orders. That is where the greatest saving potential lies. And that is also where the greatest stumbling-block lies, so you had better not underestimate that task. We have seen many start-up companies continue to struggle with such basic functions as customer billing even two or three years after their founding, especially in newly deregulated markets such as telecommunications and power. Their strong success in the marketplace is almost killing them internally. The more customers sign up the bigger the problem becomes. Over time more and more resources must be devoted to fixing the basics and no one has time to implement new functions any more. In the meantime, competitors are focusing all their energy on the core business and gaining share. So integrating your internal processes is not to be taken lightly.

Chapter 17

Real-time market research

How it can help you

Real-time market research can help you predict customer behaviour on two levels. First, it allows you to predict on a short-term basis how many modules of the options you are already offering will actually be needed. You can immediately recognize, for example, that more and more customers are ordering their PC with a particular CD-ROM and adjust your inventory and supplier orders accordingly. But real-time market research also helps you determine the kind of options that you want to offer in the future. In order to maintain and expand the existing market positions, companies have to think not only about their customers of today, but also about strategies for tomorrow.

The learning relationship with the customer can provide valuable insights into future trends that bricks and mortar companies can only obtain through costly and time-consuming traditional market research. If a product sells well, it does not necessarily mean that this is exactly what the customer wanted; perhaps it was just the best among a selection of bad choices. This is where online customization can make a difference: through the process of active customization, the customer reveals his exact preferences and provides input for market research and future product development at the same time.

> **In order to maintain and expand the existing market positions, companies have to think not only about their customers of today, but also about strategies for tomorrow**

Analyzing the data, businesses can adjust the possible choices for one product or modify the entire range offered by adding new products or dropping current ones. They can offer alternative communication channels or develop pricing mechanisms that fit the customers' needs. The key differentiator of the Internet is the extremely fast and direct communication with the end customer. Through easier, faster communication new opportunities for learning arise. The change in the marketplace becomes quicker through shorter feedback loops, leading to faster development of new products and features.

A simple example shows how the length of the feedback loop is connected with the speed of learning. Imagine you are travelling in a foreign country. In the hotel you want to take a hot shower in the morning and find yourself in front of various controls in the shower trying to figure out how to get hot water. Remember that the shower in the foreign country might work quite differently from the one you are used to at home. So you might push a few buttons or turn a few handles with one hand and check to see if there is hot water with the other.

> **The key differentiator of the Internet is the extremely fast and direct communication with the end customer**

This method of trial and error usually leads to quick results if there is a short feedback loop between your action and the result. If you turn one lever from left to right and you can feel the water getting hot the learning process is very quick and it should take you no more than ten seconds until you are happily humming a song in the shower under hot water. If the feedback loop between your action and the result is much longer, however, the learning process is significantly slowed down. Imagine that it takes three minutes instead of three seconds until the water gets hot because the boiler is far from your room. Now your chances of finding out quickly how the shower works are considerably reduced and the delay will probably be compounded by your uncertainty. By the time the hot water reaches your room you have probably concluded that this cannot be the correct lever and have turned it back and tried a few other combinations. You might even interpret the arrival of hot water as the result of something you did three seconds ago instead of three minutes ago and be quite irritated when it fails to deliver repeatable results.

The slower the feedback loop between your action and the result, the slower the learning curve. A long feedback loop makes learning by trial and error a rather annoying, error-prone and time-consuming process, in marketing as well as in the use of showers around the world.

> **A long feedback loop makes learning by trial and error a rather annoying, error-prone and time consuming process, in marketing as well as in the use of showers around the world**

The increased speed of feedback on the Internet allows you drastically to increase your learning curve about what the customer wants and does not want. But quickly finding the desired options is only the first step to gaining a competitive advantage. The time it takes to offer the desired variations is just as important in a constantly changing competitive environment. So the key is not only to find out what the customer wants quickly but also to implement it just as quickly. If it takes you one day to find out what the customer wants, but six months to implement the internal IT systems and process changes necessary, your advantage from real-time market research is not very big.

The key challenge for any player in the market is not simply to offer possibilities for customization, but to offer options that are highly valuable for specific target customers. Real-time market research helps you identify those options quickly and reliably.

Methods

There are, of course, different methods for online market research. You can analyze customer behaviour on your existing web site, such as which options they look at and which ones they actually buy.

If you run an online newspaper, for example, you can track the articles that people actually read. Newspapers that have online versions have a great advantage over those that do not which extends to their printed edition, because they know what the customers have looked at. This provides valuable information on the kind of topics that readers are interested in. Normally with the printed edition a publisher might only notice that sales drop or stagnate, but it is rather difficult to find out which articles the customers cared enough about to read.

So an online edition might actually be worth it just for the sake of real-time market research for the printed edition, although the demographics for the two might vary and therefore require adjustment.

Customer buying patterns are the next valuable source of information. Of course, any bricks and mortar manufacturer will also analyze customer buying patterns to get an idea of the products that might sell best in the future. But the information that can be obtained through the Internet offers three unique advantages that make it extremely valuable: the information is available first hand and not diluted by retail channels; it is available immediately; it is available not only for whole products but also for parts of products.

Advantages

Let us have a look at the different advantages. First of all, as has been outlined before, the Internet offers the manufacturer the unique opportunity to get first-hand information from the customer without any retail channel in between. Therefore there is no one who can dilute or distort the preferences of the customer. This is quite an important factor because today's retailers are sometimes extremely powerful and have their own agenda that may not necessarily reflect customer needs.

The second advantage is that the information on the Internet is available as soon as the customer has placed an order. This can give you a cutting-edge advantage, especially in very volatile markets because you can find out about new trends several weeks or even months before your competitors who sell through traditional retail channels.

> By constantly adjusting in real time to what customers request, the customized company can make sure that its competitors will only show up in the rear-view mirror

A third advantage is that you will be able to obtain information about the demand for individual modules of a whole product, whereas your bricks and mortar competitors will only be able to assess demand for a specific bundle of product features. Take the example of a computer built out of many different modules. The customized Internet-based company will know if customers prefer one particular CD-ROM over another and which graphic card is requested most. The bricks and mortar company selling through retail channels will only know that one particular computer model is not selling well. It will be very difficult for them to find out whether this is the fault of the CD-ROM, the graphic card, the monitor or something else. Since they only get feedback on how a complete bundle of modules sells, they have no direct access to specific customer preferences. While the traditional competitors do guesswork on why one bundle sells and another one does not, the customized company knows in real time exactly which modules customers prefer and can plan their inventory, product bundling, research and development and sales accordingly. By constantly adjusting in real time to what customers request, the customised company can make sure that its competitors will only show up in the rear-view mirror.

But what if you want to offer a new option? Previous or current buying behaviour is not necessarily going to tell you which additional options customers would like in the future. The unique characteristics of the Internet offer unprecedented possibilities to evaluate additional options. Trial and error is instantaneous, rather than prolonged.

If your product line is technically capable of producing a particular option – even at initially higher cost – you can offer a limited edition to see if there is enough demand for it. If you are not yet capable of producing the desired option, you can offer the option on your site within the product configuration process and track how many customers choose it. Within days – depending on the traffic on the site it could be within hours – the company will get a first indication of which options are most popular with customers and start concentrating its efforts on the most promising options. However, you must explain to customers that this option is not available yet and that you have offered it in order to test potential demand.

Of course, you cannot avoid the fact that some people will click the option several times. This shows again how important it is to be able to identify your customers as soon as they enter the web site because it allows you to analyze how many individual customers have clicked the option. Otherwise you might actually find that one of your competitors had employed a number of students who do nothing else but click the options you offer to lead your market research in the wrong direction and justify investment decisions that will lead to disaster.

If you still get the impression that competitors are trying to distort your market research, you can limit your analysis to customers who have already bought something on your site. Identifying customers also allows you to analyze which other products those customers have bought before. You can even analyze which options are preferred by your most loyal and most profitable customers and ensure that their future needs are met.

Of course you have to use this form of market research with care. It allows you to get very quick first estimates on demand for a particular option and can therefore be a basis for investment decisions. But if your web site is filled with options that are not actually currently for sale, your customers will usually not be too happy. So the option of just trying it out without in fact being able to deliver should be used only sparingly and be accompanied by corresponding customer information. It will also take some learning to estimate accurately what actual demand will be based on initial expressions of interest.

Trial and error can be a very successful method for trying out extensions of options or new services. Customers are usually sympathetic and will not mind if you are trying to improve your service – as long as you do not overdo it. However, this approach is not necessarily a workable option if you want to test the market for an entirely new product. If the customer has no experience with a product they will find it difficult to select options. Therefore, customization is more difficult at the beginning of a product lifecycle because customers do not know yet what they want.

The companies could also test options that are not available yet by asking the customers if they would be interested in such options, especially if the up-front investment costs for offering the option are very high. Asking loyal customers via email which options they would use in the future is not as fast as tracking behaviour on the web site, but it can also be conducted within days.

Customization is more difficult at the beginning of a product lifecycle because customers do not know yet what they want

Because gathering information online is much easier and quicker than through traditional channels, real-time market research can also be used to improve your bricks and mortar product offering. Imagine an international airline that is thinking about investing in two aircraft to serve a new route, say from Singapore to San Francisco. Analyzing previous buying patterns will lead to nothing, because, since the airline did not already fly the route, their customers who needed to go to San Francisco flew with

different airlines, about which our airline has no information. Therefore it can be quite difficult to estimate the demand for a new route. With the Internet, however, the airline could send a short email to their most loyal customers. The emails could explain that the airline is thinking about extending its service to San Francisco and could ask the customer to enter the number of times she has flown on that particular route in the last 12 months. It only takes the customer about 20 seconds to read and reply to that mail. If the mail is also connected with an incentive, say 500 frequent traveller points for everyone who answers, chances of a high response rate increase.

It will need some experience with online market research to learn to calculate actual demand from the numbers that were fed back. For example, the rate of people who did not fly the particular route at all is probably higher in the group that did not answer the mail than in the group that did answer. And people who fly that route often might not be part of your frequent traveller programme at all because they spend all their time in the air with your competitor. Therefore, numbers generated through customer email request or online click analysis have to be interpreted carefully. Nevertheless, they offer quick insights into market segments that would otherwise be very difficult to estimate.

For real-time market research it can also be important to have a one-to-one-communication relationship with at least a small group of your customers. Those customers will be more loyal but will also usually be more open with you, and are likely to give you instant feedback, good and bad, because they have a personal relationship with you.

The ability to stay on the pulse of changing customer desires and adapt to changes immediately will become one of the most important competitive advantages on the Internet. And it will become even more important if the power within the web shifts from producers to customers or information intermediaries. In that case, the individual customers or groups of customers might set options by defining exactly what they want and asking the various companies to bid for the contract. Those companies that are flexible enough to be able to deliver exactly what is requested at the lowest cost will make the deal. Most likely those will be the same companies that have already been the first in adapting to customer needs through online market research because they will be the only ones that will have the production facilities in place to fulfil the order.

> **The ability to stay on the pulse of changing customer desires and adapt to changes immediately will become one of the most important competitive advantages on the Internet**

Online market research can be used not only to design new options but also to improve other parts of the organization. Customer feedback gives the retailer a chance to obtain immediate information about the efficiency of his distribution or payment system that would otherwise take a long time.

Customer feedback therefore functions as an early warning system. This is actually nothing new but email makes it more likely that customers will respond than if they had to send a letter or telephone the call centre. A short email is much easier to compose than a traditional letter of complaint and is usually less emotionally fraught than a phone conversation with a customer service representative.

The advantages of real-time market research are, therefore, quite obvious. You can pick up trends in the market earlier than your bricks and mortar competitors and prepare accordingly. The more customers who regularly come to your site the bigger the chance that you will be able to pick up a new trend or development early on and the more customers you will gather to whom to send email queries.

In some industries a customized web site might give you the competitive edge you need for designing the standard products to fit customers' needs. But real-time market research can give you an edge over both your bricks and mortar competitors and your competitors in the virtual world as well.

The crucial variable here is the number of customers who frequent your site. If you have few customers, you have a smaller base from which to conduct your real-time market research. Therefore, it might take you longer to pick up a new trend or desire. Firms with slower feedback loops will react more slowly to changes in the demand and, therefore, fulfil demand later. Inevitably, they lose customers to sites that already offer the desired options. As soon as there is less traffic, the ability to conduct real-time market research decreases further and with it the chance to catch up again.

Any web site will, in effect, always be a series of prototypes that are continually refined and real-time market research is one of the most important tools in that process

We have discussed real-time market research in the part dealing with customized production because that is where online market research is likely to have its biggest impact. But the same techniques can also be used to check the effects of customized pricing, which we will discuss in the next part, or to optimize the customized communication, as we have discussed in the previous part. When developing a new web site, especially, continuous online feedback is critical for success. Forget the idea that you can build a web site that incorporates everything your customers could possibly want at the time you launch it! Customer desires change constantly and technological developments continuously open up new options. An Internet site that puts the idea of customization into action cannot be completely designed on a drawing board and then go live once it is finished with no further adjustment. Developing a successful customized site requires the feedback to extend or add functions that customers want. Therefore, any web site will, in effect, always be a series of prototypes that are continually refined and real-time market research is one of the most important tools in that process.

Part VI

Customized pricing

Chapter 18

Using pricing to your advantage

Pricing is an important means of influencing people's buying decisions – in fact, it is probably the most basic one. If you want to sell something – and have no care for profits – keep lowering its price and sooner or later someone will bite. Of course, there are many good reasons to lower your prices – to utilize your production capacity fully, for example, or to clear stock, or because you are in a price war with your competitors. The aim, however, is always to influence people's behaviour in your favour.

But the pricing models that are currently widespread are all based on the same preconditions as standardized products. The pricing is basically static for the same reasons that communication and product design are: if you cannot talk directly to your customer but sell through layers of sales channels, you cannot adjust your pricing to individuals because you know nothing about them that would justify a different price. You also cannot customize your pricing to individual situations in any timely way, such as low utilization of your plant, because by the time the information is processed and decisions are made and have worked their way through the retail channels to the customer, the lower utilization problem may long since be over. Unless you know a long time in advance when you will have spare capacity you cannot use the pricing mechanism as a means to solve the problem.

> **Bricks and mortar pricing models will seem quite crude compared to the possibilities the Internet offers for fine-tuning though customized pricing**

And there is another restriction to flexible pricing in the bricks and mortar world that makes it advisable to keep pricing models fairly simple: limited human capacity. If your pricing model is too complex there is a great chance that your own salespeople or the retailers you work with will be unable to adjust to changing prices. Many bricks and mortar companies are already using complex pricing models and do not always achieve the desired result. The German railways, for example, have a tariff structure that is so complicated that most of its own employees cannot understand it. Test buys revealed that in over two-thirds of the cases when customers asked for the cheapest fare from point A to point B, they paid more than the lowest advertised rate. When the trip also involved crossing into other countries, the figure rose to over 90 per cent.

This example shows that in the bricks and mortar world pricing models can very quickly become so complex that no one can handle them any more. Not only do they increase transaction costs when employees go through dozens of different pricing combinations searching for the cheapest one, they also lead to dissatisfaction and distrust when a customer gets quoted three different prices from three different employees.

When you sell customized products on your web site you will probably create a pricing model that is much more complex than most used for standardized products today. At the same time, you will rely on computers to calculate prices instead of sales agents, which will eliminate confusion and error because neither your employees nor your customers need to understand the system any more.

But even if you do not sell customized products, the Internet offers you a variety of options for advantageous customized pricing. Bricks and mortar pricing models will seem quite crude compared to the possibilities the Internet offers for fine-tuning though customized pricing.

Airlines regularly use different prices for the same product, often with as much confusion and error as the German railways. In a flight from London to Munich within economy class you will find people who have paid at least ten different prices for exactly the same product: the regular economy fare, standby, airline staff who fly for almost nothing, reduced rates for booking two weeks ahead of time, reduced rates for staying over at least a weekend, special rates for students, reduced rates for the second person, frequent traveller rewards and so on.

For the business traveller, who is usually not very price sensitive because he does not have to pay for the ticket himself, the airline wants to charge the business class or at least the full economy fare. The business traveller usually has a few characteristics that airlines use for price differentiation: he wants to be back home for the weekend, he often flies back on the same day, he never really knows when the meeting will end and which flight he will be able to catch and he usually does not know two weeks in advance where he has to go. So with a few conditions such as mandatory stays over the weekend and bookings two weeks in advance without the possibility to change anything later, airlines manage to sell exactly the same seat for five to ten times the price as the cheapest fare on the same aircraft.

The trick is to establish pricing conditions that will reduce the danger of cannibalization of different customer segments. Airlines spend a lot of resources on sophisticated capacity management. Every route is optimized individually every single day. On one flight from London to Munich on a Monday morning there might be 20 per cent of seats allocated to the cheapest economy fare, whereas on the same aircraft a week later there may not be any seats for that price because the Oktoberfest has just started in Munich and the airline knows very well that it will be able to sell every single seat for a considerably higher price. Capacity management for airlines means trying to sell every seat on every flight as dearly as possible and at the same time trying to sell all seats on each flight. An empty seat on a flight after the doors of the aircraft have closed is worth less than yesterday's newspaper, which you can always use to start a fire to keep you warm.

The trick is to establish pricing conditions that will reduce the danger of cannibalization of different customer segments

Even when planes are already fully booked with less expensive tickets, airlines will usually keep a few seats available for full-fare-paying passengers, just in case a business passenger decides at short notice that he wants to fly. So the job of capacity management is to sell every single seat in one particular plane for the highest possible price.

Clearly, capacity management based on variable pricing can yield extra profit. At the same time it can also enhance customer service. For the business traveller it is an additional and highly valued service that a certain number of seats remained unsold. And as the example also shows, even with a limited number of tools the airlines can do a great deal. The flexibility of the airlines is greatly reduced, however, by the fact that most tickets are sold by travel agents. Therefore, the airlines have to observe certain tariffs and conditions that have been communicated in advance to the travel agent. Travel agents would not be too thrilled if prices and conditions for the different tariffs changed every day. They have used the prices in advertising and all their personnel know the conditions by heart. So the airline can change the number of seats allocated to each pricing plan but cannot change the terms of each plan every day or hour. This limits the possibilities for customized pricing radically and the reason again lies in the disconnected communication structure between the airline, the travel agent and the customer.

> The customized pricing that is possible through the Internet will allow companies to realize even greater profits

Already airlines are working to put their reservation systems on the Internet. In effect the pricing will become more transparent to travellers. In general, as manufacturers talk directly to the customer new possibilities for customized pricing open up. There is no need for tariffs with rigid conditions any more because they can all remain flexible as long as there is a web site that communicates this properly to the customer. This short example shows that dynamic pricing is already commonly used today to increase profitability. In the following chapters, we show how the customized pricing that is possible through the Internet will allow companies to realize even greater profits.

Chapter 19

Reasons for customized pricing

Why should one product be sold for one price to everyone? It certainly used not to be like that. In the old days when products were made to order, the price was naturally different from product to product and also took into account variables like personal preferences and delivery time. Standard prices for commodities, price lists and so on are a consequence of the standardization process that took place during mass production and the Industrial Revolution.

Standard prices for commodities, price lists and so on are a consequence of the standardization process that took place during mass production and the Industrial Revolution

But standardized products lead not only to standardized and static prices; they also result in disconnections between producers and users. Since the manufacturer had little information about the customer, there was scant basis for customization. The retailer who sold the product had no information about production capacity and other production elements any more, so there was no reason for customization on the basis of product variation either. So standard prices developed at least partly out of lack of information and the disconnection between manufacturer and customer.

In a free market economy prices are supposed to be indicators of the scarcity of resources in relation to demand. Static pricing cannot fully compensate for these deficiencies in the short term because most prices adapt very slowly to changes of supply and demand. With the rise of eCommerce, however, dynamic and customized pricing could become the norm, especially for products where supply or demand changes regularly.

In a free market economy prices are supposed to be indicators of the scarcity of resources in relation to demand ... In the online world, the bricks and mortar limitations for pricing are no longer relevant and new opportunities emerge for customizing prices

In the online world, the bricks and mortar limitations for pricing are no longer relevant and new opportunities emerge for customizing prices. As outlined before, online client contact is rich in digitized insight into customer buying behaviour. This information, together with other customer data such as previous buying patterns or customer profitability, can be translated into customized prices.

In contrast to point-of-sale promotion or television advertisements, the Internet is essentially a one-to-one communication medium. This fact enables sellers to communicate customized prices without upsetting or alerting other buyers. Due to the dynamic nature of online customer interaction, prices can also be adjusted in real time. This gives the manufacturer additional flexibility to fine-tune his sales strategy.

The dynamic and the customized prices available on the Internet convey more information than static prices. First, the manufacturer can change to dynamic pricing, which means that he can adjust the price to the current situation. And he can customize the price, which means the price not only changes over time but might also be different for two different customers at any one time. Dynamic pricing and customized pricing are actually two different things: the first changes with time, the second with the customer. But the Internet opens up new opportunities for both types of price differentiation either one at a time or in combination, which might provide the greatest benefit.

The unique differentiator of the Internet is that all this can happen in real time. And it is this capacity to change the price in real time that gives the Internet a unique advantage over all other media. Regular retailers are physically unable to make abrupt price changes to adjust to changes in capacity utilization in the production line, but these are quite simple on the Internet. And those price tags definitely cannot be changed according to which customer happens to look at the tag. Therefore the dynamic and customized price is a more flexible tool for influencing consumer behaviour.

As with communication and customization, pricing can also be customized actively or passively. Passive customization happens if the customer selects a product and is quoted a price based on product availability, production line utilization, his loyalty and profitability and any number of other factors. Active customization takes place if the customer states the price he would be willing to pay for a certain product or service and the manufacturer then accepts or declines the offer. The other option for active customization is a setting where several customers actively determine the price as in the case of an online auction.

Dynamic pricing and customized pricing are actually two different things: the first changes with time, the second with the customer

Having the consumer state the price he is willing to pay becomes especially interesting when the web site serves as an intermediary, consolidating offers of different manufacturers. A customer could then offer to buy a flight from Dallas to Chicago for $100 on a specific date and agree to buy from any airline that can match his offer. This would be similar to a request for proposal. An airline can then accept or decline the offer.

This is a distinct advantage for the airline compared to offering the low fare to everyone. The airline might be willing to sell one particular seat on one particular flight much more cheaply than any advertised rate because that flight is unusually empty. When the airline responds to a request for proposal by the customer, it does not have to advertise the price or let everyone, especially a competitor, know that they have low capacity-utilization.

Whether prices are customized in a passive fashion through pinpointed price discrimination or whether customers set prices actively as in e-auctions or by stating the price they are willing to pay, price customization is a win-win proposition. Buyers see their individual needs and situations reflected in prices they can pay, and sellers are able to use the price as a mechanism to fine-tune sales. Understanding the potential of price customization as well as the challenges posed by it will be a key to success for online businesses.

Customized pricing can be used to achieve a variety of goals. It can be a necessary complement for customized production capabilities, or it can be used to increase traffic on a web site, enhance share of customer wallet, build customer loyalty or boost profitability.

Customized pricing for customized products

Customized pricing usually becomes necessary as soon as you start selling customized products. The customer selects the different modules or designs of the product himself, and the pricing has to reflect the different options that the customer can choose. He pays different prices for different modules, service levels, or delivery times. This is not to say that all customized products have to be sold for different prices. If you are selling jeans in different customized lengths and widths, the production costs are probably the same whether you make them two inches longer or two inches shorter. In that case you could sell a customized product for a standardized price, at least as far as the different production variants are concerned. You might still want to customize the price based on production capacity or customer loyalty.

The advantage of the Internet is that you can design much more complex pricing structures than in the offline world. No one has to understand the logic behind the structure, neither your own sales people nor the customer. People log on, click on the modules they want and you instantly prompt them with the price. If they do not like the price they can start to play around with the modules they have selected and quickly figure out the selection that best suits their needs. If the underlying pricing structure is very complicated and the choice of one module influences the price of another, it matters little because the user does not have to understand it in order to make a decision. It would even be possible to change the pricing structure every day depending on the demand curve, supply problems, capacity changes or any other reason.

But customized pricing goes further. It is more than just selling products with different modules for different prices: it is a tool in its own right. Prices can be customized even if nothing else in the company is customized.

Customized pricing to generate traffic

First of all, the mere fact that you are customizing your price will generate a certain level of traffic on your site, because of the novelty. Witness the media attention that the development of online auctions generated and you have an idea of the kind of hype that new developments in the Internet generate. And online auctions are just one of the many possibilities to customize price. The media attention that customized pricing is likely to generate in the beginning is a nice side effect, but it probably will make no sense to introduce customized pricing just to take advantage of the hype without any real business case behind it.

There are other ways apart from the media hype in which customized pricing can help you to generate traffic. As always with customization it is difficult to customize for first-time visitors, because you usually lack the information you would need for customization.

For repeat visitors the scenario is different, however. Here you already know at least a little bit about them, which will allow you to offer them specials that are adapted to their needs and are likely to get them back to your site. So if someone has purchased from your site once and has never returned, you might decide that it is time to remind them about your web site. You could send an email with a special offer that is too good to be turned down. What this means is that you are actually paying the customer to come back to your site by offering a true bargain. In principle, this is nothing new. It is exactly the same thing that bricks and mortar stores do when they offer a loss leader like coffee below or at cost. The huge difference is that the online store offers the special only to selected people whereas the offline store will have to sell the cheap coffee to everyone, including the people who just happen to be in the store anyway.

On the Internet, however, since mailings and pricing can be customized, you only have to sell the cheap product to people who you have sent the email to. All others who come to your site can still pay the regular price. This, of course, gives you an enormous advantage on the cost of such a campaign. With the greatly reduced cost you have the chance to run customer-specific specials more often and attract even more people to your site.

Naturally, the selection of people who receive such mailings and the selection of products to offer at a reduced price are both crucial for the success of such an effort. First of all you want to make sure you only send the mailing to people who have not visited your site for a while. Second, you should make sure you exclude those who always come to your site after such a mailing but only buy the special and nothing else. And third, you have to ensure that the product you are offering will interest the potential customer.

Fortunately, the information that you need for this selection is available in digitized format and once you have the necessary selection mechanism in place you can automatically select the people who have not been there for four weeks but who have a profitable buying pattern. You can automatically select the products you want to offer for a reduced rate to these particular people based on previous buying patterns. So when you generate a mailing to 10,000 people it might well be that you are offering several hundred different products for a reduced price, but each one only to a few selected customers.

You might even rely on the information that the customer himself has provided about his buying patterns. If a customer has asked to be notified if a specific product drops below a certain price, you can decide to lower the price for this particular product for this particular customer, if you think it is time for him to visit your web site again.

Customized pricing to increase conversion

Customized pricing can also be used to increase the conversion rate of those people who only surf on your site into actual customers. Imagine that you have a new potential customer on your site. From the analysis of his surfing patterns with other surfing patterns you come to the conclusion that this customer today has no intention of buying anything but is just looking around. So you offer him a coupon that takes 30 per cent off all advertised prices. The condition is that the coupon is only valid as long as he stays on the site and for a maximum of two hours. Chances that the surfer will become a customer increase significantly through this one-time offer.

In order to ensure that people do not bank on that discount and purposely surf your site in order to attract a coupon you could ensure that the coupon is only used for, say, ten per cent of all surfers who follow a particular pattern. That will make things more difficult for those who are trying to take advantage of the system. To ensure its efficiency the web site will have closely to monitor the buying patterns and profitability of the people who have been converted to customers through a one-time coupon offer.

The great advantage lies in the fact that you do not have to offer the discount to everyone but can select the potential customers who offer the highest chance for success. In the bricks and mortar world when you offer coupons, discounts or specials, you have to give them to everyone, including lots of people who would have bought the product anyway. The advantage of the Internet lies in the fact that you can carefully select your targets instead of handing out offers indiscriminately and at high cost.

Customized pricing to increase share of wallet

The mechanism to increase your share of wallet with a particular customer actually works very similarly to the mechanism for increasing traffic on your site that we have just described. You have to know enough about your customer in order to be able to cross-sell products that address his particular needs. If you also customize the price and offer the product for a lower price, it is an additional incentive for the customer, which will increase your chances of success. Of course, you do not want to cross-sell all your products for reduced prices because that would significantly diminish your profitability. But a reduced price can significantly increase the chance of a customer starting to buy from you products that he has always previously bought somewhere else.

Imagine you have a customer with a particular buying pattern. He regularly buys baby food and diapers. From the analysis of your other customers who have the same buying pattern you know that 'baby food and diaper people' usually also buy large amounts of film so they can record the progress of their little dears for posterity. However, this customer buys no film from you. And he might have good reasons for that. He might own a digital camera or he prefers to take videos of his child or he does not take pictures at all. But chances are he just buys his film somewhere else, perhaps out of habit or because he does not even know that you also sell film. You are his diaper guy, not his film guy. So next time around, surprise him with a special offer for film when he buys baby food.

You do not want to cross-sell all your products for reduced prices because that would significantly diminish your profitability

In the offline world you could also try to cross-sell by just placing the film next to the baby food. This doesn't happen too often, however, because it is not a natural juxtaposition. Bricks and mortar stores have certain physical restrictions on the goods they can place next to each other and their overall scheme for arranging goods. Placing film next to baby food will cross-sell to people with little children, but unless you are placing the film twice in your store, which uses valuable shelf space, it will make it almost impossible for anyone else ever to find the film. So one of the greatest advantages of the Internet business lies in the fact that it can cross-sell to every single customer individually. The photographer will find the film 'next to' the cameras and the proud parents will find the film 'next to' diapers and baby food.

You can offer different products to different customers at different prices, and you can even use information individual customers have given you to customize prices for them. If a customer asks you to notify him every time that a particular blend of Jamaican coffee is cheaper than $12 a pound, you could lower the price of coffee just for this one customer to get him back on the web site if you notice that he has not been around for quite some time. You would only do that, of course, if his track record shows that every time he is on the web site, he also buys a lot of other things with a high margin. You would not make such an offer to people you recognize as habitual bargain hunters.

When you start using customized pricing it becomes more complicated to calculate product profitability because you just have to account for how much you are giving away on which products and for what reasons. You may break even or even lose money. You have to find a way for your database to accommodate these variables because otherwise you may erroneously conclude that some products are unprofitable and drop them altogether, although they may actually be very effective at attracting business for higher margin products.

Before you drop a product because of low profitability you might also want to check how it sells to your most loyal and profitable customers because it may be an integral part of their shopping experience with you. And you might want to check if that product is always put in the shopping cart first when the customer visits the site, although you have done no special advertisements or mailings for it. If one or both of these criteria are met it might be an indication that the product fulfils some function in generating traffic and customer loyalty even though you have not consciously used it for that purpose.

Customized pricing to increase loyalty

Once you have generated traffic, converted the surfers to customers and increased your share of wallet you can employ customized pricing to ensure that people actually stay loyal to your site. When you are measuring customer loyalty and profitability you know exactly how much a customer is worth to you. So to cement your relationships with the most loyal and profitable people, and let the less profitable people drift away to your competitors, you can again customize the price. Giving financial rewards to your most loyal or profitable customers can even mean giving them different prices on an individual basis.

> Once you have generated traffic, converted the surfers to customers and increased your share of wallet you can employ customized pricing to ensure that people actually stay loyal to your site

In order to avoid the confusion of having two different people who know each other log on to the same site, and search for the same product and get quoted two different prices, to the consternation of one, you can always explain to the better customer that the regular price would be $5 but he only has to pay $4 because he is a loyal customer. This may lead to the second customer buying through the web account of the first, but it does not have to be negative because it actually turns your loyal customers into advocates and sales people for your product. The downside, of course, is that this behaviour limits your ability to track individual preferences and customize your service accordingly. The two factors therefore have to be weighed against each other.

From the experience with customized pricing so far, most people seem not to mind price differentiation. People on an aeroplane usually know that their fellow passengers have paid a completely different price for essentially the same service but are quite willing to accept it. The business traveller is happy that he still got a seat when booking only 24 hours ahead of time, and the student is happy to get a cheap flight at marginal cost for the airline even if she has to stay the weekend, which she probably wanted to do anyway.

You can tell the customer you are using customized pricing based on profitability or loyalty or other factors. It might seem strange at first, and will give you a lot of publicity and traffic, but after a while it will become the norm. If the customer knows you are customizing your pricing for particular reasons, it may give him further incentives to identify himself by logging on with his password or let himself be identified by a cookie to ensure he actually gets the best price. You still have to have a standard price for everyone who does not fulfil any specific criteria or if you have no spare capacity or for another reason. So the limited experience today with customized pricing shows that customers are quite happy to live with different pricing as long as they understand why it is happening.

Customized pricing can also be used to increase customer loyalty through the adaptation of the pricing to the individual demand structure of the customer. For a telecommunications company this could mean lowering prices for specific kinds of calls that the customer uses heavily, say all calls during business hours between the headquarters of the company and its three subsidiaries. Or an airline could offer the route that one particular customer flies every week for a reduced rate for that person only. This customer-specific pricing pattern increases customer loyalty. Since your competitors do not have the information about the buying or usage patterns of this particular customer, they cannot offer the same customized price.

> **Customers are quite happy to live with different pricing as long as they understand why it is happening**

Such customized pricing can also take into account the costs to serve the customer. If there are two customers with the same buying or usage pattern and one rings your call centre for bookings whereas the other books via the Internet, there are different costs associated with their behaviour. If a customer never pays his bills on time and always has to be sent several reminders before you ever see any money, the costs to serve this customer are considerably higher. If you have your IT systems in place to include these costs you can use the information to give benefits to your most loyal and profitable customers.

In the long term this can have quite significant effects on your total customer base and your profitability. With customized pricing you can offer very detailed-level incentives for the most desirable customers to do business with you instead of your competitors. This means that over time you will select your customer base and increase the share of very profitable customers. This automatically gives you a competitive advantage over your competitors. If you have a significant market share it will also have a second effect: it will erode your competitors' shares of very loyal and profitable customers, thus further increasing your competitive advantage.

For businesses that have both bricks and mortar operations and an Internet presence, loyalty programmes can be especially interesting because they allow them to capture a bigger share of wallet under one loyalty scheme. Take the example of books. Even loyal customers of an Internet bookstore will also buy some of their books in a bricks and mortar store once in a while. Reasons can vary: it can depend on the type of book, on the shopping mood, the fact that the bookstore happens to be close by or the simple fact that some readers like to browse in 'real' bookstores for some types of books, instead of just looking them up on the Internet.

> **For businesses that have both bricks and mortar operations and an Internet presence, loyalty programmes can be especially interesting because they allow them to capture a bigger share of wallet under one loyalty scheme**

If you have a loyalty programme that captures data on the sales of books to a customer regardless of whether they are bought in person or online, you can identify loyal and profitable customers better than via an Internet presence alone. Customers could have a loyalty card that they use both in a store and through the Internet.

Customized pricing to increase profitability

Everything we have talked about so far has involved special pricing to attract and keep customers. The goal was basically to increase revenue. Customized pricing can also be used as a tool to reduce costs, however, and this is what we will look at now.

Even though web site sales might be impressive, they are not necessarily the most significant or only performance measure for a successful web site because they do not capture the value that electronic commerce creates by adapting the demand curve to the production capacity. Doing so can result in significant cost savings for the manufacturer.

> **Even though web site sales might be impressive, they are not necessarily the most significant or only performance measure for a successful web site**

Pricing that aims to increase profitability by reducing costs does not necessarily have to be customized, however. In order to adjust the demand curve to the current supply, dynamic pricing would be sufficient. Whereas customized pricing varies according to the individual customer, in dynamic pricing the price varies predominantly with time. Of course, manufacturers can combine the two types of pricing. Thus, while a manufacturer may lower prices to increase the output of underutilized production capacity, he can still offer different discounts based on customer loyalty and profitability to provide the greatest rewards to his most important customers.

In a free market economy prices are the primary mechanism of balancing supply and demand. Since prices in most markets today generally change over a period of months, they cannot balance supply and demand in the short term, certainly not in the space of a few days. The necessary resources or production facilities are not in place to make immediate adjustments in output, either up or down. The result may be acute shortages or surpluses. Customized short-term pricing is a way to influence the demand side of the equation, one that did not exist on any great scale in the short-term area before the Internet.

Today in most cases when supply and demand do not match, the problem is handled on a first-come, first-served basis and through waiting lists. Any product that sometimes or always has waiting lists or requires reservation long in advance but all for the same price could profit from the use of customized pricing. This could be new cars, hotel rooms during trade fairs or theatre tickets for opening night.

Any waiting list or long reservation time is an indication of sub-optimal allocation of resources that is not based on the willingness to pay. Instead of allocating resources on a first-come, first-served basis, the retailer could adapt the price. Apart from generating higher revenue this also ensures that those customers who have the greatest willingness to pay actually get the goods or service. This can indeed be perceived by the customers as added convenience.

Customized short-term pricing is a way to influence the demand side of the equation

In Germany, someone who wants to order a Mercedes has to wait for more than a year for delivery of some models. Many customers might not be happy to wait that long and would be quite willing to pay extra in order to get the car in a couple of weeks. The actual production time of the car including the production lead time is only a few days, and the rest of the waiting period is just standing in a queue. This indicates an opportunity for customized pricing. Car manufacturers do not use customized pricing today, but the market has spawned a system that functions in similar fashion.

When there is a waiting list of a year or more associated with a new car, people will order one without ever intending to buy it. When 11 months have passed and the car has to be specified in detail for the production process, those speculators sell their right to buy the car to someone else for a higher price. This is nothing more than customized pricing. For someone who actually wants to buy the car there are two choices: she can either order the car from the manufacturer directly and wait 12 months, or she can buy from someone else for a higher price and get the car next month.

However, this informal system poses a number of problems. If the car manufacturer leaves the function of customized pricing to third parties, he loses control over the process. The manufacturer will not have access to detailed information about what his true customers really want because the customers who initially order the cars are not those who will eventually buy the cars, which makes long-term planning difficult. He also loses the chance to adjust the pricing based on customer loyalty or profitability. And he cannot avoid the danger to his brand name through the speculative activities of third parties.

The existence of such a two-tiered market shows that there is an opportunity for customized pricing to allocate scarce resources according to the willingness to pay instead of on a first-come, first-served basis.

A pricing structure that actually aspires to using pricing to bring customers' interests into line with the manufacturer's interests has to be easy to communicate. People have to be able to see the advantage in adapting their buying behaviour. If they do not know the difference between the factory price of your product and the speculator's prices in the current market, or they do not care enough to change the way they order regardless of the price, pricing changes will have no effect on the demand curve. But if they are willing to alter their thinking, they can not only get a better bargain for themselves, with the payoff either in time or in money, but also help the manufacturer reduce costs by levelling capacity utilization.

Customized pricing does challenge traditional marketing strategy

The emerging free market in electricity is a prime model. The cost structure of electrical production is largely influenced by dramatic fluctuations in demand. Utilities could considerably reduce their capacity if the demand were more level. Power companies buy and sell electricity constantly depending on whether demand from their customers is high or low, and prices can vary significantly within minutes. Unfortunately this pricing does not influence shorter term demand because end users either pay a flat rate or are unaware of the pricing changes and therefore have no incentive to adapt their consumption patterns. If utilities could come up with a variety of pricing options based on the profiles of particular companies, they might have the chance to lower costs for those companies while saving on purchases in the spot market during peaks in demand.

For example, for a company with large refrigerating units it might not make much difference if the power for the cold store is off for a couple of minutes now and then. The company could therefore set up a system that automatically adapts the consumption pattern of electrical power based on the temperature in the cold store and the current price for electricity. This would reduce cost for the power consumer and at the same time reduce costs for the power producer.

A similar approach to dynamic pricing can therefore considerably help the manufacturer to level peaks and troughs in capacity utilization, clear stock or sell spare production capacity. You can even offer the customers your products for a very low price with the condition that you will produce them some time within the next six months. The manufacturer could then produce those products at times of very low utilization, thus better utilizing his production capacity. The good thing about customized pricing is that it is rather difficult for the customer to predict when you will have spare capacity and change his buying patterns accordingly.

If you use customized pricing you must have a clear idea what your marginal costs are for each customized product, otherwise you might end up setting your prices too high or too low. And you have to ensure that you do not set pricing incentives for the customer that will lead to imbalances such as high revenues for products with low margins.

Customized pricing does challenge traditional marketing strategy, however. Since customized pricing has little in common with traditional pricing strategy, new mechanisms have to be developed to ensure that the company maintains its corporate identity. Whatever strength there was in the old identity should be maintained if possible, while creating a new basis for delivery. As we have outlined here, customized pricing can be used either to generate higher revenue or to reduce the costs to serve the customer. The actual customized price is usually a combination of both factors.

Since the Internet will boost the significance of dynamic and customized pricing, this will most likely also have an effect on pricing in the bricks and mortar world. Although it is rather difficult to establish customized pricing in the bricks and mortar world, it is likely that some of the dynamic prices that have been established for hard-to-value goods through the Internet will also be used for products and services in the offline world, because the Internet gives the manufacturer additional information about the price elasticity of the demand curve.

Passive customization

There are several different ways to use passive price customization. You can offer discounts or specials for a particular product or customer depending on when the purchase is being made, timing of the promised delivery schedule, customer loyalty or a number of other factors that have already been outlined. You can offer special deals during low capacity utilization or when you have excess stock. Different prices provide customers with incentives according to what is good for the production process.

Active customization

Price can also be actively customized by the customer himself. This can either be through negotiations with the manufacturer on a one-to-one basis or through negotiations with other customers through online auctions. On a one-to-one basis the customer offers the price that he would be willing to pay for the product. He could also specify a certain delivery period or leave some options open. The manufacturer can then accept or decline the offer.

The more options that are left undefined, the higher the chance that the manufacturer will accept the offer. First of all it will allow him to fit better into the production process if the manufacturer can choose the production time or some specific characteristics of the product. Second, the danger of cannibalizing more profitable market segments is lower if some of the options are not defined. The advantage of this option is that the manufacturer does not have openly to communicate the price he is selling for. There might be a dip in capacity utilization, but you might not want everyone else in the industry to know about it.

Online auctions offer a range of possibilities for the customized producer

Another option for active customization of price is the online auction. Here the customer does not negotiate about price with the manufacturer but with other customers. Online auctions have a few drawbacks for customization, however. The precondition for a successful auction is the liquidity of the market. If there are not enough people out there who will bid for a certain product, online auctions do not yield realistic prices, which makes them unattractive for manufacturers. Therefore, online auctions are difficult to run for products that have been customized for a particular customer because chances are that this particular customer will be the only person to bid for the product. Nevertheless, online auctions offer a range of possibilities for the customized producer.

Chapter 20

Database requirements for customized pricing

The essentials

No matter whether you customize the communication, the product or the price, you always need sophisticated database back-up to get it going. Customized pricing probably needs the most advanced database background of all customization systems outlined here because within a split second you have to take into consideration production capacity, customer loyalty and profitability, warehouse content, supplier status and many other factors. Only then will you be able to reap the full benefit of customized pricing.

Imagine that you have only the production capacity system in place but not the warehouse and the customer profitability systems. Since you have spare production capacity you could end up offering a product for a very low price not to your most loyal customers but to some surfer who just happens to be on your web site, because you do not have a clue who your most valuable customers are. Or even worse, you could offer a product with a certain specification and a certain delivery date to one of your most loyal customers for a very low price because you have spare production capacity. What if the customer buys the product and you then find out that one of the parts you need to produce it is not in stock in the warehouse or cannot be delivered in time by one of your suppliers? Missing the promised delivery date will annoy a loyal customer. And the missing part may turn up when demand is high and your production line is fully utilized. Nevertheless you have to squeeze the product in and even have to sell at the low price that you committed to. This means you will have to delay higher margin production. And so on. As the example shows, customized pricing can be a dangerous tool if you do not have all the necessary information integrated into one system or a number of interconnected systems.

No matter whether you customize the communication, the product or the price, you always need sophisticated database back-up to get it going

The same is true if you have decided to measure customer loyalty but not customer profitability. Measuring loyalty or revenue is usually much easier than measuring the profitability of a particular customer. If you have decided to take this shortcut, think twice before you use that measure as a basis for customized pricing. In extreme cases you might have a very loyal customer who buys only special offers that were meant to attract people to the web site. He has high revenue and high loyalty but eats up your margin – certainly not someone you would want to thank for his high loyalty by giving him freebies to make sure he comes back for even more.

And do not be fooled into thinking that something like customized pricing can easily be added to a web site later on. You might be able to add an auction module that runs pretty much by itself to sell surplus stock. But fully to benefit from customized pricing without getting yourself into trouble you had better have all relevant processes throughout the whole value chain integrated in one system or a number of closely interconnected systems. If the customer specifies a product on the screen, he wants to see a price and a delivery schedule at the end of the specification at the very least and again every time he changes something within the specification. The customer certainly does not feel like waiting 20 seconds until your computer systems have figured out the price. During the waiting time he might get bored and decide to check out a competitor's site.

If you take customized pricing seriously, coming up with a price for the customer involves several steps. First, you have to check if the product can be produced and delivered within the specified time. Or you could offer the customer two different prices for different delivery times depending on your capacity utilization. Then you have to check the previous buying and profitability pattern of the customer and select the customized price.

To be able to perform those functions online you need quite a sophisticated database. Imagine you have a loyalty function based on revenue in your web site that is already up and running with fixed prices. Then you decide that it would be a good idea to introduce customized pricing based on that loyalty.

> **Do not be fooled into thinking that something like customized pricing can easily be added to a web site later on**

Within the whole database set-up, price has always been used as a fixed number that could be stored and looked up in a table. Now you suddenly want to make the pricing of a product a variable within the whole database. To make pricing variable based on production utilization could still be done manually. As soon as we are talking about different prices for every customer, the whole system has to be set up to accommodate this feature. So a lot of reprogramming has to be done to ensure that the price can realistically be adjusted according to the criteria you want. Once you have finished, you may find out that customer loyalty is actually not a very good basis for customized pricing and that you would prefer customer profitability.

If your loyalty programme is equipped to measure only revenue, integrating customer profitability means a redesign of large parts of the database. From the customer perspective nothing has changed in the whole process. The customer knows only that there is a loyalty programme and that he is quoted a certain price for a certain product. The example underlines the importance of designing the database from the start to integrate the mentioned features, even if they are not used in the beginning.

Price differentiation, therefore, is a powerful weapon, but it can become a double-edged sword. If you are not sure you are capturing customer profitability correctly then you had better not differentiate price based on customer profitability. If you are not sure your production management shows you the actual times of low capacity utilization you had better not run specials for certain times because you might not be able to handle the demand that this generates. This may sound obvious, but you would be

> **Price differentiation is a powerful weapon, but it can become a double-edged sword**

surprised how many companies out in the bricks and mortar world base their decisions on approximated product or profit centre profitability that cannot withstand thorough scrutiny. The more you are trying to use pricing to differentiate and fine-tune your processes, the more you have to be sure the numbers you use are a valid basis for your decisions because the customers will react promptly to any changes in the incentive structure.

Chapter 21

Auctions as a means of customized pricing

Through the Internet, the possible uses of auctions multiply. The geographical reach is practically unlimited. Lower cost items that would not justify a terrestrial auction can find large numbers of buyers. The electronic infrastructure removes constraints regarding volume, variety and time. Auctions share the real-time nature of price negotiations. In auctions, bidders can specify the price they are willing to pay. The result is an actively customized price. Since price is the single matter at issue, auctions can deal with large numbers of bidders simultaneously.

Internet auctions are currently built largely on the entertainment effect that stems from real-time pricing. Auctions conducted by Lufthansa, for example, are not primarily used for the purpose of selling off spare seat capacity or customizing price, but have more of an entertainment value. Very few seats are actually auctioned compared to the spare capacity in airlines. It is a promising prototype, however, because it may help the airline learn about the preferences of its customers and develop its site accordingly.

The electronic infrastructure removes constraints regarding volume, variety and time

But apart from their entertainment and publicity value, there are other economic reasons for using online auctions. Online auctions reduce transaction costs because buyer and seller in different parts of the world find each other more easily. The negotiation mechanism also helps save time and reduce transaction costs because the price is the only variable. Since pricing is part of the transaction the bidder reveals his willingness to pay in the course of the pricing process. This fact renders online auctions attractive for pricing products and services with significant valuation uncertainty.

Valuation uncertainty stems from a variety of factors. If fluctuations in supply and demand are significant, if there is a shortage of comparable goods, or if private values determine buyer valuations, it is extremely difficult for sellers to set the right price. Auctions offer a good alternative for determining price. Auctions capture all factors that determine willingness to pay. Real-time, interactive pricing does not require a predetermined price, but relies on market forces. However, for auctions to come up with a realistic market price, the number of bidders has to be large enough to ensure the liquidity of the market.

Internet auctions are currently built largely on the entertainment effect that stems from real-time pricing

In the bricks and mortar world auctions have been used mainly for high price, hard-to-value items such as art works and antiques or items that had to be sold quickly, such as houses. Products were auctioned because of market illiquidity, because of unsteady supply, or because they were non-standardized with high value. On the Internet, these factors still apply. But auctions can now also be used for lower value items because of reduced transaction costs and because of the large number of potential participants. Auctions are, therefore, especially suitable for goods where it is difficult to determine a fixed price due to situational or product-inherent factors. There are three categories of products that are particularly well suited for selling through online auctions that can be identified: commodities, time-sensitive goods and used, outdated or damaged goods.

Commodities

Some products are auctioned to determine a fair market price in a fluctuating trading environment with volatile pricing. Several online auction services have already established themselves in metal, energy, and livestock trading – all of this is really an extension of existing exchanges and, in the case of livestock, the kind of regional auctioneering that used to be a feature of rural life.

The auction becomes the clearing mechanism for commodities where supply and demand fluctuate too much to use fixed prices. Another example is car rentals. Demand for convertibles changes significantly with the weather forecast for the weekend. Instead of long reservation times, car rental companies could auction the convertibles they have available at short notice, say the Friday night before the weekend.

Time-sensitive goods

Auctions are also a viable clearing mechanism for time-sensitive goods such as unused capacity or perishable goods. They often face erratic supply and demand. Online auctions can help clear these goods quickly by setting appropriate clearing prices. Examples include spare seat capacity on airlines and underutilized production capacities. Time-sensitive goods have a value of zero as soon as the time is up. An empty seat in an airliner, a month-old bushel of tomatoes, or last week's excess production capacity have a value of zero. Time-sensitive goods lose their value with the passage of time. Therefore, the most important feature of the auction is the speed of the clearing mechanism. Many products or services will fall in both the commodity and the time-sensitive goods categories. In the case of energy, it is both a commodity and a time-sensitive good.

Used, outdated or damaged goods

Used, outdated, lower quality or damaged goods are often sold in consumer-to-consumer auctions such as eBay. But they also gain relevance in the business-to-consumer or business-to-business trade. Ingram Micro, for example, auctions off several million dollars' worth of overstocked inventory to its customers per month. Online auctions help price these goods which lack a viable market price. Dell Computers uses its web site to auction off used PCs that have been leased to corporate accounts. The auction serves two functions: it sells off used inventory and it generates traffic on the web site. If a customer cannot find what he is looking for chances are that he will check out details and prices for a new PC instead of a used one.

Auctions can also be an interesting option if you offer customized goods but at the same time offer a 'no questions asked' return policy. You might end up with a considerable customized inventory that would otherwise be hard to sell. Auctions can be a good mechanism to sell those customized goods. The value of these goods is hard to determine, since they have been customized for one particular person.

In the business-to-consumer market auctions are a powerful way to sell off items directly, address bargain shoppers and provide entertainment to consumers. In the consumer-to-consumer market online auctions have a bright future as a substitute for classified ads.

Auctions can be used together with customized messages. A potential buyer could be informed by a customized message that the product he was looking for is now on auction. Auctions are more difficult to use in conjunction with customized products, however, because when the product is customized for one particular person there is no point in auctioning it, because there will probably not be enough people who want to bid. Here it might be better to use other means of price differentiation as outlined in the previous chapters.(Auctions can, however, be used to sell off customized products that have been returned to the manufacturer, as noted above.)

In the consumer-to-consumer market online auctions have a bright future as a substitute for classified ads

Any product or service sold through an auction has to be clearly described before the auction starts. For damaged goods this is difficult, but not for customized goods, because the web site explains all the customization options in order to sell the new goods.

There are different basic types of auctions. In seller-led auctions the auctioneer is directly involved in the transaction as a seller. He runs the auction to increase sales or sell spare capacity. In third-party auctions the auctioneer is not directly involved in the transaction process and lives on a commission. In buyer-led, reverse auctions the auctioneer is directly involved in transaction as a buyer and is interested in low prices. Of course, sellers and buyers do not necessarily have to run the auction themselves. They can use a third party. Regardless of who runs the auction, the differentiating criterion remains whose interests count most. In the case of the seller-led auction, the aim is to sell every single product or service for the highest possible price, but still sell it. In the buyer-led auction the aim is to buy every product for the lowest possible price but still get it. In both cases auctioneers can optimize price, realizing lower purchases or higher revenues.

Value-added features of online auctions include automatic bidding up to a certain price, email notification of bidding status, and bidder ratings based on previous transactions, especially in consumer-to-consumer auctions. Proxy bidding can be used for extended auctions. The bidder can specify how he would like to bid, such as limits up to what price or increments, and therefore does not have to take part in the auction the whole time. Another format is the moderated auction, where the bidders not only specify the price but can also add comments to their bids. Bidders use the additional comments to get each other going and might be inclined to bid higher than they originally intended 'just to show' the other participant. This is an interesting feature especially in business-to-consumer and consumer-to-consumer auctions.

Auctions can also be combined with other means of customized pricing. When auctioning spare seat capacity for flights, the auction could be run for everyone, but if a frequent traveller happens to bid on the seat he could receive a discount on the auction price.

There are other types of customized pricing that involve the participation of a group of people but that would not traditionally be called an auction. Some features can only be produced economically when volume reaches certain levels. What is economically possible depends not only on the costs of the production process but also on the prices customers are willing to pay.

Imagine that a car manufacturer has a machine to paint cars which requires a good deal of time and money to change between colours. He would therefore set up the production process to use the same colour for as many cars in a row as was possible. Nevertheless, he can still customize the colour. For all people who have just signed the contract for a new car that will be delivered in a couple of weeks, the car manufacturer could run a colour auction. The customer could make a selection from several hundred colours and set the price he would be willing to pay to get that colour produced. That price determines how many other people will have to be willing to pay the same price until the selected colour will be produced on a particular schedule. The individual would

Customized pricing has to be very closely linked to the actual production cost in order to fully reap the benefits

only pay a price that might be lower than the one he has offered to pay. As a result people might pay different prices for different colours. If 100 people have chosen orange they will pay less than the 30 people who have chosen pink.

This kind of pricing only makes sense if the production process has the limitations outlined earlier. If the painting machine is capable of painting every car in a different colour at no additional cost, the free choice of colour could simply be included in the customization options for the product without any additional charge. The example shows again that customized pricing has to be very closely linked to the actual production cost in order fully to reap the benefits.

Part VII

Outlook

Chapter 22

The future and your options

As the technical infrastructure becomes increasingly abundant and new technical possibilities offer greater opportunities for adapting to the needs of individual customers, the focus of competition shifts towards the creation of customer value through customization. As in the bricks and mortar world, knowing your online customer is the single most important requirement for success. What is different is that in the online world customer information is digitized and can cost-effectively be taken apart and put back together to create a customized shopping experience.

In the past information technology has had to be aligned with the company's business model. Technology was forced to fit the business model. In the world of the Internet the technology becomes the driving force and many times the business model has to be adjusted to the new technical options.

Throughout this book we have described the different possibilities that customization can offer and we have shown the tools that can be used for customization. Every company can use those tools in different ways to support its particular business model or strategy. Your choice of tools depends entirely on your particular situation, business, product and target customers. As technology evolves it creates new opportunities and customization will evolve accordingly. The three facets – customized communication, production and pricing – can be employed in combination or separately. Even if you feel that the particular product you are selling cannot in any way be customized, you can still customize your customer communication and pricing.

> **As the technical infrastructure becomes increasingly abundant and new technical possibilities offer greater opportunities for adapting to the needs of individual customers, the focus of competition shifts towards the creation of customer value through customization**

The book has outlined the possibilities for customization. It has shown a direction in which companies can go based on the possibilities that are available today. This is not to say that we have described everything that is possible today. There are other possibilities we have not looked at and that perhaps nobody has even thought of yet. But looking at the web sites available today (and that includes taking a look at your own!) you will be among the top web sites if you implement only half of the things we have suggested. Now that the technical infrastructures for customization are there and the idea has been developed, every company can choose one of three basic options.

Option 1: Attack

A company can incorporate the ideas we have suggested and start to become a customized enterprise itself. If done properly it will ensure that most of your competitors will only show up in your rear-view mirror. The first-mover advantage does not make it impossible for others to catch up even when starting late, but they will face an uphill struggle. Many bricks and mortar companies are afraid of starting a customized Internet business, however, because they are worried that it might actually be successful and cannibalize their other business. But just think again: the real choice is cannibalize or be cannibalized.

Option 2: Defend

You can choose not to start a customized business yourself but to prepare instead for the fact that current competitors or other players will incorporate the idea of customization and prepare your response to these changes in the competitive landscape. Since the technical infrastructures are available today it is only a question of time until someone starts to use them. And it does not have to be one of your current competitors. Just imagine for a moment what would happen to your industry if a company like Microsoft suddenly decided that it will take part in the game. For industries such as banking this idea is not far-fetched and might give some executives more than just a shiver up the spine.

> Since the Internet offers a distinct first-mover advantage, starting second in the market is, in most cases, not an appealing option

Since the Internet offers a distinct first-mover advantage, starting second in the market is, in most cases, not an appealing option if you have a choice. You may want to choose to leave the first-mover advantage in the mainstream of your business to others and concentrate on a niche market that is not influenced by customization today. Or you might want to see which mistakes the first mover makes and avoid them when you start yourself. But be aware that the first mover may define the new business by its action, whereas you, as the number two entrant, will be gearing up to be mistake free in a shrinking old business. In many cases analyzing how you could react to others starting a customized Internet business will lead you to the conclusion that it is far better to choose option 1.

Option 3: Do nothing

Finally, the company can ignore both of these options and continue to do business as usual – and commit commercial suicide. The time of its extinction will be determined by the speed with which other companies move towards customization on the Internet. The principle of survival of the fittest remains unchanged.

> Continue to do business as usual – and commit commercial suicide

Index